101 Things Every New Dad Needs to Know

Everything You Need to Know to Make

Fatherhood a Breeze

Hayden Fox

Claim your free gifts!

(My way of saying thank you for your support)

Simply visit **haydenfoxmedia.com** to receive the following:

- 10 Powerful Dinner Conversations To Create Amazing Kids

- 10 Magical Affirmations To Help Kids Become Unstoppable in Life

(you can also scan this QR code)

Table of Contents

Introduction

Listen, there is no way any true man is going to let children live around him in his home and not discipline and teach, fight and mold them until they know all he knows. His goal is to make them better than he is. Being their friend is a distant second to this.

- Victor Devlin

So, you're a dad; what now? Or maybe, you're not officially a dad *yet,* but your partner is expecting, and the clock has started ticking!

Regardless, you're a dad in spirit, whether or not the practicalities have caught up, and the one thing that's certain is that you're determined to be the one that your precious child deserves.

I understand how you feel, and I know all about the overwhelm that's now washing over you. I also know how desperate you are to pull your weight and do your bit, having quite literally watched your partner carry the load for the past nine months—no matter how many foot and back rubs you might have given!

The thing about doing your bit, though, is that you need to know precisely what bits need doing, don't you?

As a father of three kids, I know exactly how you're feeling. I have faced the conundrums, seen the tantrums, and shed the tears that parents endure while striving to do the absolute best for their children.

One thing this book won't have to teach you is that our children need our absolute best; the decisions that we make when they are at such a tender age are absolutely critical for their future. Hard work, blood, sweat, and tears (and trust me, there will be lots of tears!) will all be required, but no one thought having children would be easy, did they?

Disclaimer: If you *did* believe that having children would be easy, then you were sadly mistaken! And if you're thinking to yourself "Well, I was easy to raise! I was an angel! My parents had it easy." You, my friend, are what we like to call a historical revisionist.

Parenting is hard, for everyone. However, it's the things that are the most difficult and that pose the greatest challenge that are the most rewarding, and I can assure you that raising children will be the most rewarding challenge you will ever face!

What makes challenges easier? Help. And that's precisely where this book comes in!

I wrote this book to be a go-to resource for new dads. A resource that you can trust and rely on and that offers practical and actionable advice. Put simply, this book is *the* resource that I wish I had when I became a dad. So, in a way, you're already ahead of the curve. I'm actually kind of jealous…

Within this book, you will find an abundance of

- advice.

- insight.

- support.

- tips.

- resources.

We'll cover a wide range of topics that span from pregnancy to infancy and include categories such as

- bonding and development.

- navigating fatherhood.

- newborn care.

- feeding and nutrition.

- helping out during the pregnancy.

- sleeping strategies (for you and your baby).

- health and safety.

- the important role that a father plays.

- dealing with tantrums and the ominous word "no."

- the importance of keeping your cool, as well as allowing yourself to blow off steam.

This will ensure that you finish this book feeling much more prepared, confident, and equipped! That way, you can stop worrying and embrace the excitement of what's to come.

All of the information in this book will also be accompanied by a healthy dose of research, evidence, facts, and figures. However, the most helpful reference points that I can truly give you are the real experiences that I have gone through. I have also sourced information from the army of dads around me—although some of my own dad's advice might be a little... iffy! We can learn from each other's mistakes and triumphs and combine this with scientific knowledge to create our own version of fatherhood tailored to best support our partners and babies.

There is truly no greater gift than the gift of life; so grab a coffee, settle in, and let's get you through this next big milestone of your life together, shall we?

Welcome to *101 Things Every New Dad Needs to Know!*

Chapter 1:
Helping Throughout Pregnancy

Being a father starts long before your baby is born. It starts with being there for your partner throughout the duration of pregnancy and afterward.

- Anonymous

Fatherhood is a journey, so let's start at the very beginning. No, not *that beginning (get your mind out of the gutter!)*. I'm talking pregnancy. Those of you who have already witnessed the terrifying yet beautiful miracle of childbirth, feel free to flick ahead to Chapter 2, *and give yourself a pat on the back for not passing out in the delivery room.*

There's no way around it, Dad, you're going to feel a little helpless during this period; but fear not, there are plenty of ways that you can help your partner!

Become a Sponge

Be prepared to get really porous.

You'll be receiving information from everyone in your life, and I truly mean *everyone*. Your parents, siblings, friends, doctors, your parent's doctors, your friend's siblings, and so on and so forth.

Your partner will, of course, want to take everything onboard too, but as the pregnancy progresses, they're only going to become more tired and uncomfortable, so we can forgive them for finding information retention a little more challenging.

That's where we come in!

Be sure to take notes, grab leaflets, and absorb everything you can. I know you're inclined to just nod your head and think to yourself 'I'll totally remember all this! 'I'm here to tell you that having a baby, isn't exactly the same as your Freshmen year English final. You can't cram last minute. Be diligent!

The more you learn, the greater a job you'll be able to do when your partner is apprehensive or concerned about something.

Information isn't the only thing you need to be prepared to absorb, though. Remember the tiredness and discomfort I referenced earlier? Well, that's going to come with some side effects, such as your partner being incredibly cranky and short-tempered.

Who can blame them; they're sharing their body with another human!

Your secondary role as a sponge—and this will be tough at times—is to absorb that crankiness and stress. Let them be slightly short-tempered, ignore the comments about the fact that you didn't do the dishes, and just absorb. Although, if you can, for the love of God, just do those dishes. It's for everyone's wellbeing.

Cut them some slack, and let them be as grumpy as they want. Besides, who are we to judge? We won't know what's it's like until we grow a human inside of us for nine whole months. Think about it. You just shuddered a little bit, didn't you? Exactly.

Preparing Your Sleep Pattern

Remember when I told you that this book would provide you with advice outside of the theoretical guidance you'd find online? This is one such vital practicality.

I know you love your sleep, who doesn't? But the reality is babies do not care about that…like at all. So, you've got to prepare yourself for a new sleep pattern! Sounds fun, right!?

Talk to your partner about how things are going to work with regards to sleep schedule, and if you'll be doing a share of night feeds—which I recommend that you do, despite work commitments, as it's a great bonding time with your child. Then, start preparing your body for these adjustments now.

I know that most of the commonly touted advice surrounding this says to get as much sleep as possible before your baby is born, but you have to consider the shock that this will cause to the system when that amount of rest can suddenly no longer be your norm. I was told the same thing, and it led to a huge, inevitable level of burnout once my children were born.

If the plan is to alternate night feeds, then around seven months into the pregnancy, it is helpful to start getting up in the middle of the night for 15 minutes; set your alarm early, and shift your body so that early nights become the norm.

It's not all bad. You get to spend some time watching TV at 3am. Hope you like reruns!

I can feel you rolling your eyes at me right now. Stop it! I promise this is for your own good.

Become Your Partner's Personal Assistant

We've already covered how justifiably grumpy your partner is going to be, and another way that you can really take the pressure off them is by becoming the PA of your household.

If you've ever had an internship, this isn't much different. But instead of grabbing coffees and scheduling meetings you'll be…Okay you'll pretty much be doing just that, but this time it's actually rewarding!

You'll have lots of appointments to keep up with and pre-birth classes to attend. Don't leave those commitments to your partner; buy yourself a calendar, hang it somewhere you can see it every day (I recommend the fridge), and write *everything* on it.

I have friends who don't trust themselves to read the calendar, so they have all kinds of alerts and reminders set up on their phones, which can, of course, be a big help too!

Also, bear in mind that your partner might not want or feel like they need this help. Don't patronize them or try to wrestle any control from them that they are comfortable with; just make sure that you have your own calendar too.

They'll thank you when they let something slip and you're there to subtly remind them of a commitment.

All in all, just make sure to try your best and be a support system for you partner. This is the one PA job, you WON'T want to get fired from!

Babyproofing

Right now, the thought of being able to hold your baby, let alone watch them crawl and make their way through the house, feels a long way off, but it really isn't.

The earlier you can start babyproofing your house, the better. This allows you to check one thing off of an ever-increasing task list, giving you some peace of mind.

A few examples of ways to babyproof your living space, include:

- installing locks on your cupboards.

- fitting stairgates to not only your stairs but your kitchen door too.

- blocking power outlets with covers.

- tidying up any loose cords or wires.

- rearranging any breakables that are within reach.

Some of the above might seem obvious, but you will be amazed at how quickly your baby develops from a little bundle staring back at you to a crawling and climbing little explorer!

Remember that when you chose to have a baby, you agreed to open up your home to a fragile human that needs protecting, so no matter how much you love your display of baseball trophies on your television cabinet, it might be time to build a shelf for them.

One way of assessing your babyproofing is getting down your own hands and knees and taking on the role of your baby!

Crawl around and consider what things might catch your child's eye. What things are at ground level that they could hurt themselves with?

Just be prepared for this experiment to be documented via video camera by your partner, and shown to everyone you know and love. The things we do as fathers!

Equipping Yourself

You're going to need *a lot* of new equipment for your baby. Don't let yourself become overwhelmed. Make sure that shopping for these items is fun, and that you and your partner do so together. This is a great time to build excitement together and to continue bonding as a couple too.

Full disclosure: Once you start shopping, you're going to be tempted by everything you see. Everything will look adorable and, thus, be deemed essential in the moment. They aren't, and your budget won't thank you for this impulsiveness!

I promise you, that $200 designer diaper bag can wait!

Try to stick to the essentials first, such as

- a baby bathtub.

- a car seat.

- a crib.

- fitted crib sheets.

- a changing table.

- a diaper pail.

- a baby monitor.

- a Moses basket.

- a baby bouncer—okay, so this one is not quite essential, but kids love them!

While we're on the subject of essentials, I'd like to offer a word of advice about clothes: As mentioned, you will find every single item that you see adorable and want to buy all of them. But here's the thing, the first clothes that you buy will be grown out of so fast that if you buy your child a lot of outfits, you probably won't even get to see them wear them all!

And let's not forget babies tend to be a bit...messy. That cutesy-wutesy onesie you bought may just end up being covered in baby barf after just one wear.

I recommend exercising some restraint and buying the following:

- 6 onesies or baby grows

- 6 shirts

- 6 pairs of pants

- 6 pairs of one-piece pajamas

- 2 rompers

- 2 jackets or sweaters

- 5 pairs of booties or socks

- 2 newborn hats

- 2 swaddles

- 1 fleece suit or bunting bag

- Baby tuxedo (fine, fine you don't actually need this one, but wouldn't that be so cute!?)

Most of you simply won't be able to show the restraint I'm recommending—I certainly couldn't—but consider yourselves warned! So, I leave you with one last piece of advice when it comes to shopping: up your credit limit.

But seriously, please make sure you install your car seat ahead of time; don't leave it to one side with the false sense of security that you'll *get to it,* they can be a pain in the ass to put in and you can't bring your baby home from the hospital without one!

Plan the Route

When the time comes, your partner is going to need you to be an ocean of calm while she panics on pregnancy island.

Of course your initial reaction will be "OH MY GOD! OH MY GOD! IT'S HAPPENING! WHAT DO I DO!??"

Which is valid, but isn't really helpful.

One of the best ways that you can help yourself, and her, is by knowing the route to the hospital or birth center that you'll be heading to when the time comes.

Obviously, this isn't necessary until the third trimester, but once you're in the end game, you should check that you don't just know the route but are also aware of any shortcuts. You could even take things one step further and put the route in your satnav ahead of time. Then, once the time comes, all you'll need to do is press one button, and you'll be able to concentrate on driving safely and responsibly to the hospital.

It may seem like a lot, but it sure is a better alternative than taking an Uber to the hospital. You want to preserve that 5 star passenger rating, don't you?

Pack a Pregnancy Bag

Whilst we're on the subject of the third trimester, another important job that you should do ahead of time is the packing of a pregnancy bag. Seriously, Dad, the absolute last thing that you want to be doing while your partner is in labor is rushing around and throwing things into a bag.

Full disclosure: Your partner may want to pack this bag themselves, but that doesn't mean that you can't offer to do it or help them with it. The more you can take off their plate, the more supported they'll feel.

Of course, to pack said bag, we need to know what needs to be packed! I recommend packing a backpack or over-the-shoulder bag (to keep your hands free) and fill it with the following (*Pack Your Bag for Labour*, 2020):

- relevant hospital notes

- your baby's birth plan

- three sets of loose clothes for your partner during and after labor

- nursing bras if your partner will be breastfeeding (don't guess, ask them!)

- multiple pairs of comfortable underwear for your partner

- maternity or sanitary pads

- a toiletries bag that includes

  - a toothbrush

  - a hairbrush

  - a flannel

  - soap

  - deodorant

  - hair ties

- towels

- their favorite books or magazines or a device that they can use to pass the time and relax

- loose fitting nightwear, such as a nightie

- a dressing gown and slippers

- healthy snacks and drinks

- a onesie for your baby

- the outfit you want to take the baby home in

- loads of diapers (just in case!)

- bibs or muslin squares

- a blanket

Don't be afraid to ask your partner about anything you're not sure of; they'll appreciate your desire to be involved, I assure you.

Side note: While all of the above might not be relevant for anyone planning a home birth, I'd still recommend putting everything together, either in a bag or a cupboard, so that you have everything you need to hand when labor starts!

Exercise Together

You're in this together!

Any doctor who knows their stuff has probably already recommended you and your partner complete a 10k footrace by the second trimester. What? You didn't know that? Told you parenthood wasn't easy.

No, I'm totally kidding. However, gentle exercise is great for mother and child but also for you. So, be sure to not only encourage your partner to take walks but to join her too. You could plan your walks as part of your daily routine, and use them to strengthen your relationship and share your excitement for what's to come!

An exercise that I recommend throughout the pregnancy is swimming, as the water will support your partner's weight and ease the pressure of the baby on her joints (*Swimming in Pregnancy*, 2023).

When it comes to swimming though, be mindful of water that is excessively hot or cold (sorry, that means no jacuzzi time), and make sure your partner doesn't go crazy; no excessive twisting or turning, and make sure you're the only one doing any cannonballs!

Bond With Your Baby

No, this isn't in the wrong chapter!

Did you know that your baby can hear your voice from 24 weeks after conception? Make sure you talk to your baby plenty so that once they're born, they'll recognize Daddy's voice.

Now, I'm not suggesting you perform Shakespearean monologues for your child every night, unless of course you want them to come out of the womb with an affinity for old English which is...kind of awesome?

Instead, get into the habit of saying good morning and good night. Allowing your baby to familiarize themself with your voice will begin the development of the beautiful bond that you will share.

Carry the Load

Do you know what we dads really, really underestimate during our partner's pregnancy? Just how heavy our babies can become and how much of a strain that weight can place on Mom's body.

Have you ever had a burrito that was just a liiiiittle too big? And you felt kind of bogged down all day? Okay, think of that, times it by ten, and then deal with it for nine months. Yeah, not easy!

You might call me crazy here, but I promised you that this book would include a nice dose of advice from real dads, and here it goes: A few of my friends—I won't pretend to have tried this myself—brought themselves wraparounds that they placed weights into, in correlation with the weight of their baby. I've been reliably informed that not only was the constant weight completely exhausting, but a couple of them could barely make it through the first day.

I recommend this strategy for two reasons:

1. You'll have even greater empathy for your partner.

2. It will put a smile on your partner's face.

Give it a try, and have fun with it!

Maintain a Healthy Diet

Did you know that us dads commonly gain weight alongside our partners during pregnancy? And unlike our partners, we have no physical excuse!

Dads gain an average of 14 pounds throughout pregnancy for multiple reasons, including stress and changes in our hormones and testosterone levels (Coleman, 2022). In my case though, and no doubt in the case of many, the problem was simple: I was giving in to her cravings too. (P.S. pickles with ice cream is actually not that bad, don't knock it till you try it!)

The last thing that we want to do is ignore our partner's pregnancy cravings, but the more junk that there is in the house, and the more takeout ordered, the more we're going to be tempted to eat it too.

This a problem though, as once our baby is born, they are going to need us on top form, not winded walking up the stairs! Try to maintain a healthy diet, while supporting your partner's cravings, and remind yourself that you're not just maintaining your health for you anymore.

Utilize Pregnancy Apps

We live in a world where there are apps for everything, and that includes having a pregnant partner!

From apps like Daddy Up—which provides words of advice from other dads and offers hints and tips to supplement this book—to HiDaddy—which talks to you as if it's your little one and suggests things that you can do, like listening for the heartbeat, feeling kicks, and a countdown to the due date— apps offer a wide variety of pregnancy support and information. There's a fancy app for whichever stage of pregnancy your partner is at, and many of them are tailored specifically to a dad's experience, so get scrolling through the app store!

And of course, who could forget DoorDash! The app that will allow you to fulfill your partner's craving for pancakes at 2 o'clock in the morning. Don't you just love the future?

The Birth

There are no words I can actually give you to prepare for the birth itself, whether it's your first child or your fifth, no pregnancy is the same, and the combination of wonder and fear that each one brings will feel equally overwhelming.

This section looks at the role that we can play when the time comes, but before we get into that, here's a quick piece of advice: Prepare to feel helpless.

When it comes time, and your partner is in labor, there's every chance that they may not even realize you're in the room, which is why the most important thing that you can remember is to be a calm, constant presence for when your partner needs you.

Don't worry about racing around and trying to provide drinks, help the medical professionals, or squeeze on your partner's hand. Just concentrate on giving them precisely what they ask for, even if that's shutting up and doing nothing!

It is vital that you learn to sit with the discomfort of having no control of a situation before the birth because the more uncomfortably helpless you feel, the more likely you are to *try* and help, even where help isn't needed.

Take a backseat, let the professionals do their job, and listen to what your partner needs. I have friends who spent the majority of their partner's labor reading or watching something on their tablet because it was the only way to stop them trying to interfere and stress their partner out more!

Remind yourself that you have a massive role to play, just not right now, and come prepared with methods to keep yourself out of the way.

In the next chapter, we'll move on to some newborn

strategies to help you when you get your partner and baby home.

Chapter 2:
Newborn Strategies

Nothing ever fits the palm so perfectly, or feels so right, or inspires so much protective instinct as the hand of a child.

- Gregory David Roberts

This chapter will provide some strategies to help you with your new bundle of joy!

Establish a Routine as Soon as Possible

The sooner you establish your daily routine, the better chance you have of regulating your baby's sleeping and eating patterns. The more regularly your child is eating and sleeping, the happier they, and you, will be!

Don't be fooled into thinking that you'll have a crumb of control in this regard, though. The key is learning your child's routine and adjusting to it quickly. They are in control! If you thought your boss at work was bad, oh just you wait!

You'll soon learn how often your baby wants to eat, which

can be in anywhere from one- to four-hour intervals. Learning their patterns will allow you to prepare the bottles ahead of time, minimizing the time your poor baby needs to yell at you that they're hungry! And believe me, they have no problem yelling at you.

The more frequently you change your baby's diaper, the less chance they have of developing diaper rash, so I aimed to change my newborn's diapers every two hours—unless they intervened with a little present for me, of course, made with extra, extra, um...love.

Then, there's the sleep schedule. Again, your newborn will be in charge here too; once they show you what time they naturally start to fall asleep, stick to that time and facilitate a routine.

Once bedtime has been established, you should stick to that time every night, even on the nights that baby wants to play. You could also help them self-soothe, by placing them in bed when they are tired, but not asleep, and providing them with a nighttime routine.

We'll talk more specifically about bedtime next!

Let Your Baby Sleep

Did you know that for the first five months of their life, a baby needs anywhere between 16 and 20 hours of sleep a day? They won't ever sleep like that again! Well, until they become teenagers that is.

Think about it: In the womb, there was no day and night, or light and dark; they were cozy, warm, and dark, all day long!

Focus on making their days as active as possible, with bright sunshine and energy, and ensure that the nights are as boring and quiet as possible.

How to make the nights more boring? Watch golf, read an algebra textbook to them, listen to NPR. The world is your boring oyster.

Try to remember that though babies sleep a lot, they also wake up a lot too. Some may even move and make little noises every 30 minutes or so, but that doesn't mean you should be tempted to scoop them up every half an hour. Leave them to settle themselves back down again. This will prevent them from relying on you to do so later.

When it comes to your child's crib, keep it free of any stuffed animals or toys, bumpers, or blankets. Stick to a fitted sheet and a nice light-up mobile hanging to help settle them down.

Dress them in comfortable, warm clothing for bed, such as a onesie, but avoid anything loose fitting.

Babies should also always sleep on their backs to reduce the risk of sudden infant death syndrome.

One final, vital note on sleeping: Regardless of how tired you are, and despite how warm and cozy you and your baby are together, you should never let them sleep on your chest; it's dangerous, and there's no circumstance where this is safe.

Skin Contact

Skin-to-skin contact is crucial in helping you to bond with your baby from a very early age. It also helps regulate your baby's temperature and heart rate, so whip your shirt off at every opportunity and get your little one on your chest—just remember to do so safely and at the right time and place! Going shirtless for skin-to-skin at the local McDonalds? Yeah, that's a big no-no.

I found that the best times for this were during night feeds and immediately after waking up in the morning. Before you get up and the craziness of the day starts, grab a few moments of skin contact with your baby.

A friend of mine decided that having a baby meant that he should also commit to living in his underwear, and he spent the entirety of his paternity leave semi-naked so that his child was getting lots of contact with him. And though I wouldn't specifically recommend that, his heart was definitely in the right place!

Become a Chatterbox

I've always been a big talker, so this strategy came naturally to me: Every single word that your child hears from a young age serves to strengthen their relationship with you—as they realize, *So, that's who I could hear when I was in that cozy womb!* (Or, if you went with my Shakespeare idea from earlier they're thinking *Verily, 'tis the voice that did resound within yon cozy womb!*)

Oh, that reminds me. Speaking to your child also helps them start to develop their speech and language skills.

Your baby wants to hear from you. Your voice is familiar and a source of comfort, so just hearing from you is enough to encourage and soothe your child. Pretend that you're providing a running commentary of your life, and have at it! Think of every day as one of those nature documentaries.

"And here we see now, the adult male, going off three hours of sleep, cautiously approaches the fridge, as to not wake his sleeping mate"

I spoke to my kids all day, every day, from telling them that I was doing the dishes to describing the birds outside or even trying to indoctrinate them into liking my favorite sports teams—that one may get an eye roll or two from your partner.

Don't be put off by your child's lack of verbal skills, they're listening!

Pay Attention to Cues

Though your baby won't be able to communicate verbally right away, that doesn't mean they won't be telling you what they need.

I'm not going to pretend that every single gurgle, coo, or cry has a specific meaning. But the more attention you pay, the quicker you'll be able to attribute those noises, and even facial expressions, to one of the big three needs that a newborn baby , or a very drunk person, requires:

- a diaper change

- a feed

- sleep

Early on, that's really all that will concern your baby, and it won't take long for you to differentiate between the lovely coos of happiness that they give you and the grumpy grunts of hunger or tiredness.

When it comes to a diaper change, your baby might strain or even sigh with relief when they're done pooping (we've all been there). Hunger signs might include smacking their lips or sucking on their hands, whereas tiredness can be shown by a glazed stare or jerky limb movements.

The better you get at reading your baby's cues, the more prepared you'll be to settle, feed, or change them!

Breastfeeding

Just in case you weren't paying attention to any of the pre-birth appointments, or like 4th grade science class, you will not be breastfeeding your child. You may be wondering why even have this section at all?

Well, that doesn't mean that you can't support your partner throughout the process. This support can come in the form of little things like back and chest rubs, bringing them pillows or water when they are supplying milk, or even just reassuring them and being right there alongside them.

Try not to see breastfeeding as your partner's job; though your role is certainly not equal to theirs, providing support is still crucial. Anyone who has asked their partner about the experience of breastfeeding knows that it can be a pretty horrible task filled with chafed and split nipples, being bitten extremely hard, and babies simply refusing to latch while screaming out of hunger.

Unlike the wraparound technique there is no way for us to understand what this feels like that isn't wildly inappropriate. So, just use your imagination, okay?

Be there for your partner in any way that you can, and always encourage them to express their milk into a bottle so that you can take care of the night feeds without having to wake Mom up too; they'll thank you for the rest.

Get Playing

You might think that playing with your baby is, well, to be blunt, a little pointless in the beginning. But even when they aren't really moving, their brains are on the go constantly, and they're absorbing everything!

Your baby may not be ready for Chess, or Texas Hold 'Em, unless of course they're a genius baby, in which case why are you even reading this book? Point is, none of this means they still can't play!

By dancing, singing, tickling, or showing them brightly colored toys, you are helping to stimulate their ever-developing brains and exciting them too! Read things in a silly voice, pull funny faces, and have fun! Your child will feed off of your excitement, and even when they don't show it, they'll feel excited too.

And let's face it, dads. Those baby toys? Kind of fun for you too, you gotta admit!

Other ideas that will help you play with your newborn, include:

- smiling, sticking your tongue out, and pulling faces that your child can eventually try to copy.

- shaking rattles.

- providing your child with brightly colored toys to focus on, which will also help develop their ability to focus.

- reading brightly colored books to your baby.

- swaying to soothing music with your baby in your arms.

- quietly singing lullabies to your baby.

And then, there's tummy time! Lay your baby on their tummy so that they can flap their arms and legs playfully. This will help them strengthen both their shoulders and neck muscles. Just remember to supervise them at all times, and help them out if they get frustrated; it's supposed to be fun, after all!

Schedule Family Visits

Something that most people don't tend to think about is the sheer amount of people that are going to want to come visit your baby.

Suddenly a great aunt three times removed who you didn't even know existed will be coming out of the woodwork to see the precious bundle of joy. Sorry parents, you're old news, chopped liver, the baby is the star of the family now!

Just remember that you're going to be very tired, and your baby is only going to be awake for a certain amount of hours in the day. You're also going to have so much going on that scheduling all of these visits will probably be more than you need to have put on your plate.

Always ask visitors to check before popping over; one easy tactic to employ when you have the support of extended family is to ask both sets of grandparents to co-ordinate their planned visits together to take it out of your hands. In my case, I was incredibly grateful to have a friend who was willing to be designated as the planner for these visits, scheduling them within slots I'd already approved. Rather than going back and forth with multiple people, I was able to simply receive one text telling me who was visiting and when!

Once guests do arrive, be honest with them about the duration of the visit if you're too tired to play host, and don't feel the need to get yourself shaved and groomed either!

Also brace yourself for everyone's family members' favorite pastime, giving unsolicited parenting advice! You get a point every time you hear "When I was raising (insert child's name of said aunt who is three times removed you barely know here) we did THIS!"

You'll reach 100 points in no time!

That in mind, if having visitors feels like it's going to stress you out, hold off on them until it doesn't.

Get Yourself and Baby Out of the House

Okay, so, in the first few months, it's going to be easy to just bunker down, lock the doors, and stay inside. That's understandable, but you have to remember you're a new parent, not a doomsday prepper. Outdoor time is essential!

My advice to you is to get yourself out into the world as quickly as you can and rip that Band-Aid off!

Don't be shy about taking your baby to a restaurant; just make small adjustments, such as checking that your table will have enough room for your car seat or stroller, asking for the check to be brought to the table with the food, and packing your bag appropriately so that you aren't stuck without any necessities!

If the only way of getting yourself out is by planning to go during your baby's naptime, then plan to do so, bringing them with you while they snooze in their car seat or ensuring that your partner will be home to look after them.

You should continue to do the things you enjoyed before your baby's birth, within reason. I don't think happy hour at your favorite bar is the best place for a newborn. Unless you get them fake ID of course.

When they are awake, your baby will also love getting out and seeing the outside world, and you will love seeing them react to the wonders of it for the first time!

To you, it's just a regular, everyday garbage truck. To them? It's like seeing the Grand Canyon! A Grand Canyon that smells awful, but a Grand Canyon nonetheless.

While we're on the subject of seeing the wonders of the world, I also want to take this moment to reassure you that you don't need to worry about flying either. Despite the stigma around babies on planes, babies sleep so much that it's much easier to plan a newborn's sleep schedule around long-distance travel than it will be when they're a toddler (that's when they learn this fun little trick called 'Hey! Let's see how many times I can kick the back of the seat in front of me)!

Don't feel trapped in your home; your baby will sleep just about anywhere, provided you plan ahead!

Diaper Changing

It's everyone's favorite part of parenting! Okay, I can't even say it as a joke. Let's be real, diaper changing is not fun. But, some evils in this world are necessary, and this is, unfortunately, one of them. But don't worry, I'm here to help you through it!

The first time you change a diaper, chances are you'll be very intimidated, but you'll be changing them one-handed while on the phone in no time—I'm kidding, don't do that!

The first thing that you can do to help yourself is to gather all of the required bits and pieces before you remove the dirty diaper So, keep the following by your changing table:

- a changing mat or towel

- lots of packets of alcohol- and fragrance-free baby wipes

- a plastic bucket or bag for the dirty diaper and wipes

- barrier cream

- lots of clean diapers

- clean clothes in the case of an explosion

- And maybe a nose plug for the explosion mentioned above.

It is also helpful to have a ready-to-go diaper bag filled with more of these essentials for when you leave the house. Preparation really is key here; so, make sure that you have all of the above to hand before you even consider pulling the tabs on your baby's diaper! That is the type of mistake you make once and once only in your parenting career. Let's shoot for zero, shall we?

In the beginning, you might even want to lay everything out in the order that you'll need it to prevent any confusion or overwhelm. Then, gently lay your baby down onto their back on the changing mat, and remove any clothing from below their waist that is restricting diaper access.

Open the diaper with the two front tabs, then use the clean front part of it to wipe any loose poo from your baby's bottom. Gently lift their bottom up to release the dirty diaper, and place it in your prepared bucket or bag. Then, use the wipes to clean your baby.

Next, comes the clean diaper: First, check that it's the right way around—sticky tabs to the back. Then, slide the back of the diaper under your baby's butt. Apply a little barrier cream to your baby's genitals and bottom, and then, pull the front of the diaper up—ensuring that your baby's penis is pointing down where necessary—and secure it using the sticky tabs on either side.

All that's left to do is to dress your baby again, putting clean clothes on if the old ones have become messy!

Oh, and...please wash your hands afterwards.

Washing and Bathing

If you have a nose, you may notice that your baby can get a little stinky. Hey, happens to the best of us. We'll go over more specific bath routines for toddlers later, but let's focus on washing your baby when they're still infants.

Let's start with bath time itself: You'll want to use a baby bath and lukewarm water in a warm room. A baby bath will come with a special backboard to lay them on, but they should never be left in it on their own.

Be sure to wash your newborn baby in clean water, free of any bubbles, and avoid submerging their head. My equipment of choice was a cloth that was not only soft but also tickled a little too!

Once you have lifted your baby out of the bath, gently pat them dry, and pay special attention to all of their lovely creases!

Your baby doesn't have to be bathed every day, unless they really enjoy it! For those who don't want to bathe their baby every day, another option is *topping and tailing*. This is just as effective as a bath for your baby and is as simple as using damp cotton balls to gently wash them from head to toe on their changing mat. Just remember to use a fresh cotton ball for each part of their body and pay close attention to all of those folds when you're drying them!

Next, we'll move on to some specific sleep strategies for your newborn to help you both get your 40 winks!

I just heard the sighs of relief from every exhausted father reading this, didn't I?

Chapter 3:
Sleep Strategies

That moment when you go to check on your sleeping baby and their eyes ping open so you drop to the floor and roll out of the room like a ninja.

- Anonymous

This chapter will take a look at some sleep strategies for your newborn, as well as moving through the baby stage towards toddler age. Before we go any further, it is important to note that the strategies within this chapter are all options for you to explore; every baby and parent is different, so move forward with the strategies that show progression, and feel free to discard the rest!

Let's start with some strategies for the immediate future.

Babies

Check and Console

You might also see this strategy called "the Ferber method," "the interval method," "progressive waiting," or "graduated extinction."

Whatever fancy name you choose to give it, the key here is to check on your baby at consistent intervals, and do a little consoling—verbally or with something like a gentle touch on the arm or a squeeze of their chunky little toes.

The rule here is that no matter how upset or worked up your baby might be, you can't pick them up! Once you do that, you tell them that their crying has worked, and they'll start to rely on you to rock, or feed, them to sleep.

So, how does it work in practice? Once your baby is settled in their crib, leave them alone for around a minute; then, pop your head back in and give some reassurance (verbal, or physical). Every time you leave the room, increase the time interval before checking on them again, going from, say, one minute to three minutes, then up to five, and so on.

Once you reach between 10 and 15 minutes, stop increasing,

and stick with regular intervals until they fall asleep. If they wake back up, start the whole process over again.

This particular strategy may take up to a week to show results, but if your baby takes to it and you're comfortable with it, it can be a game-changer. I recommend keeping a sleeping log to reassure yourself that it's working on the evenings when it feels as though it isn't—and yes, unfortunately, there'll be a lot of them (Gagne, 2020).

Cry It Out

If the check-and-console method isn't working—or to be blunt, if it appears to be p*ssing your baby off more—then you might need to consider letting your baby cry it out. This is called "the full extinction method."

I know it can be hard. It feels evil, cruel, and like you're more of a supervillain than a loving father. But unless your name is Lex Luthor, I have good news! You're totally in the clear. This technique is very beneficial for you and the child.

After taking your baby through their bedtime routine, kiss them goodnight, place them in their crib while they're still awake, and leave the room. The next step is the one that is a little controversial, and to be honest, its effective implementation all comes down to how strong you and your partner can be.

One strategy requires you to leave your baby to cry until they tire themselves out and fall to sleep, with the only exception being attending to them during their scheduled night feeds, of course!

An alternative method suggests that once your baby has woken up twice, it's okay to go in and give them a little reassurance (without picking them up!), before leaving again until they have twice more self-soothed to sleep and woken up again.

Look, guys, this method is going to suck, and the first night is going to be one of the worst nights of your life; I'm not kidding.

But for babies that take to this method, it can be a fantastic way of ensuring that you get some sleep and they learn to self-regulate. The best part is that for babies that do take to this method, results will often happen after just a couple of nights. Trust me, your future self will be thanking you for this!

However, this method is not recommended for babies whose parents need to be separated from them a lot during the day, such as in the case of guardians who are forced to return to work very quickly after the birth. Where a child does not have ample opportunity to see their parent(s) meeting their needs at other times of the day, the cry-it-out method can contribute to lifelong patterns of anxious attachment.

Nevertheless, where it works, this method works *very* well; so if your circumstances allow for its healthy implementation, it is definitely worth a try. If it's working, each night should bring less and less crying, but if it isn't, try to stick with it for one to two weeks to give your baby a fair chance at adjusting before switching strategy (Gagne, 2020).

The Chair Strategy

This strategy might take a little longer than some of the others in this chapter and is another one that I'm reliably informed can be very hard in the beginning. Hey, I told you in the very first chapter, fatherhood isn't for the weak!

This time, once you have settled your baby in their crib, you should relax in a chair right beside it. Don't worry, once they fall asleep you can leave the room, but if they wake back up, you return to the chair and give some gentle reassurance, without picking them up!

You may be there for awhile, so make sure to invest in a chair that is comfortable, AKA now you finally have an excuse to buy that recliner you've been eyeing!

Every couple of nights, you can move the chair further and further away from their crib, and preferably closer to the door, until you can remove it from the room completely!

This can be hard because not only can your baby see you, and potentially become more desperate for your affection, but you can also see your baby crying; so, allowing them to self-soothe can take even more restraint than usual.

On the other side of the coin, however, you are, of course, present to offer verbal reassurance, and just your presence might provide a source of calm.

I know dads who have tried and hated this method and dads who tried it reluctantly but were delighted by the results. Just remember that all of our babies are different! If you find your baby becoming more distressed and don't see any meaningful results after a fortnight, move on to a different strategy (Gagne, 2020).

Pick Up, Put Down, Shush-Pat

This strategy is more effective for babies younger than seven months and requires you to stay in the room with them but refrain from giving them too much help.

You can stand over their crib and reassure them with gentle shushing, patting their tummy, or gently squeezing their feet. Or you might prefer to let them cry until they start to escalate, then soothe them in your arms for a little while, making sure you return them to their crib before they fall back to sleep. The key is that they need to fall asleep in their crib, rather than in Daddy's arms.

As mentioned, this strategy is most effective with younger babies because after seven months there will be an increased risk of your presence stressing your baby out, (and let's face it, who wouldn't be stressed out from another person, ten times their size, standing over them while they sleep?) and frequently picking them up might confuse them (Gagne, 2020).

Bedtime Routine Fading

Implementing this strategy is all about gradually reducing your presence in whatever method you have been using to help your child fall asleep, until you no longer have to be a part of your baby's sleep routine.

If part of your baby's bedtime routine involves you rocking them in your arms until they become sleepy, simply start doing it less and less from night to night. Maybe, you read them a story or have a timed mobile that dances above them; in this case, simply read them a shorter story or turn down the timer on the mobile.

This strategy can be hard to sustain, partly because we love reading or rocking them! So maybe pick a book you hate reading! May I suggest your old college textbooks collecting dust in your attic?

But seriously, this strategy not only has the potential to reduce the time your baby spends crying, but it will also help your baby to sleep independently, meaning that you can too!

Bedtime Hour Fading

Different from the above, this strategy specifically relates to your baby's bed*time*—as in, the time that they typically start to drift off.

The first step is to work out what time your baby tends to fall asleep. You can do this by setting up a baby camera—I recommend a Tapo—and keeping a diary for a couple of nights. Just make a note of the exact time that your baby nods off; then, start putting them to bed at that exact time.

Once they adjust to going to sleep right at bedtime, rather than after it, you can start to adjust their bedtime in 15-minute increments, until you reach the time you would like them to go to bed.

For instance, let's say that you usually put your baby to bed at 7 p.m., but they don't sleep until 8 p.m. That suggests that their natural bedtime is actually between 7:50 and 8 p.m. So, you could start putting them to bed at 7:50 p.m., and then, gradually move back towards 7 p.m. once they have adjusted to falling asleep at bedtime (Gagne, 2020).

Savor these moments, dads. It won't be long until they start bargaining for later bedtimes.

Before we move onto some toddler-centered strategies, allow me to provide a bonus tip for those of you with babies: They find white noise incredibly soothing!

Toddlers

Involve Them in the Routine

A bedtime routine is crucial, particularly at the toddler stage of development. Try to be consistent with their routine, starting things at the same time each evening and completing them in a set order that tells them it's time to wind down.

The specifics of the bedtime routine that you implement will vary depending on your child, of course, but I recommend a few quiet activities that start to calm their active brains down in the lead-up to bedtime. For my sons, this looked like

1. 7:00 p.m.—a warm bath.

2. 7:20 p.m.—a nice massage before putting on pajamas.

3. 7:35 p.m.—warm milk.

4. 7:45 p.m.—brushing teeth together.

5. 7:50 p.m.—getting into bed to listen to me reading a story.

This may vary depending on your children's preferences, but the key is to provide familiarity, comfort, and routine.

It's also important that they're involved every step of the way. This prevents them from feeling like they're being dragged to bed and empowers them to feel that they're going willingly, setting them up for positive lifelong sleep habits!

You could let them choose their favorite bubble bath, the pajamas they want to wear, or the cup they want their milk in. You could also encourage them to squeeze the toothpaste out onto their brush. (Just be sure to have some paper towels ready if you do)

Plant the Seeds Early on

Getting your toddler to go to bed at a reasonable time is about much more than just their bedtime routine. In fact, from the second they wake up, you're essentially planting the seeds of their routine for that evening.

This has many different elements, including ensuring they get the right amount of physical exercise throughout the day, with the UK's National Health Service recommending three hours of exercise for a toddler each day (*Physical Activity Guidelines for Children*, 2018). If that sounds like a lot, bear in mind that the three hours include all of the time they spend running around the living room, and they don't have to be filled with specific exercises.

Believe me, once you get them to walk, you can't get them to stay put. Toddlers put us to shame when it comes to getting our daily steps in.

Then, there's nap time. Naps are vital for toddlers, and getting them wrong is setting yourself up for failure. At this point, some books would throw more statistics and sources at you; I'm not going to bother with all that, I'm just going to hit you with some first-hand experience that I learned the hard way: Naps are good before three years old, and it's okay for your toddler to nap for anything up to two hours, but do yourself a favor and prevent them napping past 2 o'clock to ensure that they can still sleep at bedtime. After three years, my kids stopped napping unless they were ill. Some children still nap up until they're five years old, but keep them strictly before 2 o'clock. Any naps after 3 p.m. are what we call "danger naps;" you've been warned!

Lastly, there's the "small" issue of screen time. My advice to you would be to keep your toddlers away from the stimulation of technology after dinner to allow their brains to calm naturally.

I know, I know, you're getting invested in your toddler's favorite show, just as much as they are! But I promise, that next episode can wait until tomorrow.

Soften the Blow

Let's talk about the transition from playing to bedtime and how much it sucks for toddlers. Think about it, they've been having a great time with their toys and Daddy; they're stimulated, they're buzzing, and then, everything stops.

It's the toddler equivalent of the bartender shouting out "LAST CALL!" Not fun. They aren't happy about it, and who can blame them?

There are things that we can do to soften the blow and prevent that transition from feeling so harsh. Involving them in a consistent routine will help, but how do we get them to willingly step into that routine?

One of the things that I found the most effective was letting my kids include a toy or two in their bedtime routine with them. If they have already been playing with a toy, instead of wrestling it from them (sometimes, literally), let them take it with them in the bath or play with it while you're massaging them.

I've even let my kids take their toys into the bedroom with them on particularly troublesome nights and only taken the toy away once they were drifting at the end of their bedtime story.

Full disclosure: Regularly allowing your child to play with their toys in their room until they fall asleep isn't recommended in most parenting books, but I've done it in emergencies, and I'd do it again. When necessary, bend the rules!

Restrict Your Toddler's Bedroom to Sleeping

Your toddlers are flooded with stimulation throughout the day, like music, bright visuals, voices, tastes, and smells. Remember that at their age, everything is amazing, and they're seeing things for the first time on a daily basis.

That can be amazing but also overwhelming, so it's really important that when it comes to bedtime, their brains are able to settle and slow down. Therefore, the last thing that our toddlers need is more stimulation when they get into bed!

I get it; you want your toddler's bedroom to be a vibrant and fun place that's packed with some of their favorite toys, and you want it to feel unique to their tastes. It's their room after all.

Now, I'm not saying the walls have to be gray and the place needs to look like a penitentiary. However, the problem is that all of those toys can excite them, and rather than just relaxing and going to sleep, they will end up actively fighting the urge to play with them.

I recommend keeping a toy box in the bedroom so that all toys are out of view, except for a few cuddly toys on the bed and some books for bedtime reading. When it comes to nightlights and music boxes, I've found the most success with those that are on a timer.

On top of this, if you can avoid letting your children play in their bedroom and reserve the room for winding down, your toddler will see the room as a peaceful environment, rather than be confused or wanting to play.

Yes, your lounge will look like a bomb hit it most days, but your toddler's sleep pattern will thank you for it!

Staying Strong

This next strategy is similar to the "cry-it-out" strategy from the baby section above. It aims to build sleep independence through the removal of parental support after bedtime.

Unfortunately, though, this strategy is much harder with a toddler and can make you feel absolutely awful, to be honest; but don't return to your toddler's bedroom unless they are in danger of hurting themselves. The second you return, you're justifying their screaming, and it will only get subsequently worse.

Once you know that your toddler is safe, use a baby monitor or camera to keep an eye or an ear on them, and leave them to self-soothe. The absolute best thing that you can do for your child is to stay strong until they cry themselves to sleep and learn that bedtime truly means bedtime.

If you're looking for a cold, hard strategy to get you through this time, I have only one, and that's cracking a beer once they've settled—provided that it is safe to do so, of course—and reminding yourself that the second your toddler wakes up, they'll have forgotten all about it!

In the next chapter, we'll move on to strategies that we can utilize to keep our children healthy and safe so that we can focus on having fun and aiding their development!

Chapter 4:
Health and Safety

Choosing to concentrate not on ourselves but on making sure our babies grow healthy, stay safe, and are happy is worth the sacrifice.

– Anonymous

Chapter 4 will look at some strategies to keep our children healthy, and safe—what could be more important than that?

Babies

Handling Your Baby With Care

Handling your baby for the first time can be a nerve-racking experience. You're worried about hurting, or worse yet, dropping them, and you end up handling them like a bomb disposal expert by keeping them at arm's length!

Once you've gotten over the first few "OH MY GOD, THEY"RE SO FRAGILE!" Panic attacks you'll realize that while you don't have to be *that* careful, caution should, of course, be exercised; but don't worry, I've got you.

The first point worth mentioning is that you should always clean your hands thoroughly with hand sanitizer before handling them, and make sure that everyone else does too! Your baby's immune system will be weak initially, so ensure you aren't passing them any germs. Think about all the stuff you've touched throughout the day. Let's be real, humans are gross. Your baby isn't quite ready to handle said grossness just yet, so this step is very important.

For the handling itself, always support their head and neck, as they won't be able to yet! Treat that head like a fragile little egg, and be as gentle as you can, cradling it when carrying your baby and supporting it as you lay them down. I can't stress this enough: Their necks aren't strong enough to support their heads yet!

Side bar: You'll know when your baby's neck is strong enough because they'll show you. But still, remember to give them all the support they need, and act as though they can't support their head until they leave you in no doubt that they can!

There are a couple of important tidbits that I'll also touch upon now for my own peace of mind: *Never* shake your baby—not out of frustration, not to wake them up, not to get them to sleep, and not even during play. Avoid any kind of rough play until they start to grow stronger!

Soothing Your Baby

Soothing your baby the right way is important to not only calm them down and make them feel comfortable but also to ensure they feel safe.

The world is foreign and scary to them. Think about all the times you've had to experience something new, like your first day of work. Bet you wish you had someone to soothe you then too, huh? Although, having your father rock you back and forth at the office may lead to a trip to HR…

Some ways of doing this include giving them a nice massage, working from their feet up to their head; just be mindful of the soft spot on their head, and always massage very gently.

Another great way to soothe your baby is through sounds. Noises like cooing, babbling, blowing raspberries, and blowing kisses are great calming influences, as is some gentle music or a musical mobile. Full disclosure: My kids were soothed by me playing rock music at a low volume, so it's never too early to share your favorites!

Be mindful, though, as some babies may be more sensitive to sound, light, or touch. If they seem startled or distressed or appear to turn away from sounds, make sure to keep light and noise levels low.

Sorry, dads. The father & son/daughter rave events will have to wait until they're older!

Swaddling

Another great way to soothe your baby is swaddling. Due to the importance of swaddling safely and how easy it is to get it wrong—which I did multiple times—I felt it was important to give it its own section.

The goal of swaddling is to keep your baby's arms close to their body, giving them warmth, comfort, and security. Swaddling can also help to minimize the startle reflex, allowing them to sleep peacefully.

To swaddle safely, follow these steps (Ben-Joseph, 2018):

1. Spread out a baby blanket, slightly folding one corner.

2. Lay your baby down on the blanket, face-up, with their head above your folded corner.

3. Wrap the left corner of the blanket over your baby's body, bringing it under their right arm, and tucking it gently beneath their back.

4. Bring the bottom corner of the blanket up over your baby's feet, pulling it gently towards their head.

5. If the blanket gets too close to your baby's face, fold it down.

6. Don't wrap the blanket too tightly around their legs, leaving their knees and hips slightly bent and turned out.

7. Wrap the right corner of the blanket around your baby, tucking it under the left side of their back, and leaving their head and neck poking out the top; if they look like an adorable baby burrito, you've done a good job!

8. Slip your hand between the blanket and your baby's chest to check that there is room for comfortable breathing and that the blanket isn't loose enough to come undone.

Note: Swaddling should stop when your baby starts to try and roll over, which is typically around the two-month mark; rolling over while swaddled can be very dangerous.

Umbilical Cord and Circumcision Care

Though the latter won't apply for all babies, both umbilical cord and circumcision care are important enough to be included here.

Umbilical cord care can be pretty daunting and look a little gross—you know that I'm right. When it comes to the umbilical cord stump, the area around it should always be cleaned with plain, clean water and then blotted dry. Avoid putting too much pressure on it, and when you bath your baby, avoid any pools of water forming in the belly button area.

The stump should fall off between 10 days and 3 weeks after birth. If it starts yellow and then begins to look like a dried up piece of black beef jerky that's been sitting in the sun for five years. Don't panic! It's completely normal. Apologies for the visual, by the way. But, be sure to call your doctor if you see any discharge, if it's giving off a foul smell, or if it looks red and inflamed.

After your baby has been circumcised, doctors will typically apply a little petroleum jelly and some gauze to ensure the wound doesn't stick to their diaper. Again, this can be daunting, but after you've changed your baby, gently wipe the tip of their penis clean with warm water, rather than a baby wipe, and apply a little petroleum jelly with some gauze.

Any irritation of redness around the area should heal within a week, but if things aren't healing, appear to be worsening, or blisters start to form, then call your doctor immediately (Ben-Joseph, 2018).

Dressing Your Baby Appropriately

Dressing your baby can be tricky, and it can be easy to get wrapped up in what looks damn adorable, rather than dressing them in the layers that they need. Remember that while our babies need more help to stay warm than we do, they can also dehydrate quickly if they're too hot, so a balance has to be struck! So, it looks like those adorable baby mink coats you may have seen at the mall, aren't the best choice. Sorry to disappoint!

Let's look at the different times of the year, and how they will affect your baby's clothing.

Summer

Babies under six months should always be kept out of direct sunlight, so a wide-brimmed hat is always a good idea. (Plus they look so darn cute in them! Like little baby beach grandmas!)

In the heat, a single layer of breathable, lightweight cotton should be enough to keep your baby cool and stop them overheating.

It is also worthwhile to consider a clip-on sunshade or parasol for your baby's stroller, and avoid covering it with a muslin blanket which will increase the risk of your baby overheating!

At night, if the weather is really hot, you could even leave your baby to sleep in just their diaper or a short-sleeved undershirt.

Winter

In winter, it's a good idea to dress your baby with one more layer than you are wearing. If there's a chill that requires you to throw a sweater over your t-shirt, your baby will probably need a cardigan over their onesie and t-shirt.

Our babies can't regulate their temperature very well, so any hats or clothing that they're wearing for warmth should be taken off the second you get into somewhere warm—yes, even if it means waking them up; otherwise, they'll get too hot.

At night, resist the urge to wrap your baby up too much, which will risk them overheating. Instead, stick to a sleepsuit or a snuggly sleeping bag. Always favor extra layers, such as a sleepsuit, over extra blankets, which might risk suffocation.

Always remember that a cool baby is safer and healthier than a hot baby, and they'll look adorable no matter what they wear. So much so that you'll find yourselves taking daily photos to show your friends and family. Don't worry, every new parent goes through the "paparazzi" phase.

Regulating Your Baby's Temperature

If the previous strategy has taught us anything, it's that your baby's temperature is important!

It's first important to think about ways to check your baby's temperature; how exactly will you know that they're too hot? There are a few hints, the first of which is checking their tummy. If they're hot to the touch, strip some of their layers off or take off some of their bedding. Remember that folded blankets count as two or more layers. If their tummy is cold, add another layer. But don't panic if only their hands or feet are cold; it's perfectly normal!

When it comes to room temperature, anywhere between 60

and 68°F is safe, and should make your baby comfortable, along with some light bedding (*How to Dress a Newborn Baby*, 2023).

Don't worry about putting extra clothes on your baby when they're unwell or have a fever, and try to remember that babies should *never*:

- sleep in direct sunshine.

- sleep next to a fire, radiator, or heater.

- sleep with an electric blanket or a hot water bottle.

Choking

If you're anything like me, your child choking is one of your worst fears and something you'd rather not consider, but it's really important to be prepared in case the worst happens.

Let's start with babies: Make sure you always hold your baby's bottle while they're feeding, even when they are able to hold it themselves; always stay with them and keep an eye on them. When your baby is able to eat solids, cut their food up as small as possible, and never take any chances. Grapes—a favorite in my household—should always be cut lengthwise!

You can never be too careful! But if you find yourself chewing your kid's food for them, well, you may have gone just a step too far.

Children under four should never be given hard foods like whole nuts or boiled sweets, and they should only eat under your supervision. Make them sit down. This may be a challenge, but sitting with them and preventing them from running around while they eat will drastically reduce their choking risk.

Unfortunately, food isn't the only thing that your children are going to want to put in their mouths, they apparently find things like pennies, LEGOS, batteries, etc. to be delicious. Who knew babies had such sophisticated palates?

So be aware of any small items. If they're small enough to be put in your child's mouth, keep them out of reach!

Now, let's look at how we can help our children if the worst were to happen: Your first step should be removing the object from your child's mouth if you can see it, but never poke blindly as you'll risk making things worse. If your child is coughing loudly, encourage them to keep doing so, but if their coughing isn't working, it's silent, or they're struggling to inhale, stay with them and shout for help from others.

If your child is still conscious, and their coughing isn't doing the trick, your first step should be back blows.

Back Blows for Children Under 12 Months Old

1. Sit down.

2. Lay your baby face down along your forearm or thigh.

3. Support their head and back with your hand.

4. Deal up to five blows to the middle of the back (between the shoulder blades) with the heel of your hand.

Back Blows for Children Over 12 Months Old

1. If your child is small, lay them along your forearm or thigh as you would a young baby and deliver the blows.

2. If your child is too big for this method, support them in a forward-leaning pose, and deliver the five blows with the heel of your hand in between the shoulder blades

If back blows don't relieve your child's breathing, and they're still conscious, the next step is to try either chest thrusts (for babies under 12 months) or abdominal thrusts (for those over 12 months).

Chest Thrusts for Children Under 12 Months

1. Lay your baby along the length of your thigh, face up.

2. Place two fingers in the middle of your baby's breastbone.

3. Push five times sharply to compress your baby's chest by around a third of its expansion.

Abdominal Thrusts for Children Over 12 Months

1. Kneel or stand behind your child.

2. Place your arms under their arms and around their upper abdomen.

3. Place your clenched fist between their navel and ribs (avoiding their lower ribcage).

4. Grasp your fist with your free hand.

5. Pull sharply upwards and inwards five times.

After the Chest or Abdominal Thrusts

- If the object is still stuck, and your child is conscious, restart the sequences above.

- If you're still alone, call out for help.

- Always stay with your child.

- Call 911 on speakerphone to keep your hands free.

- Even if the object has dislodged, seek medical help in case part of the object is still stuck or your child has been injured by the thrusts.

If Your Child is Choking and Loses Consciousness

- Lay them on a flat surface.

- Shout for help.

- Call 911 on speakerphone to keep your hands free.

- Open your child's mouth and remove the object if it's clearly visible and safely within grasp.

Toddlers

Injury Prevention

Your toddler is going to get themselves into all kinds of trouble, it's almost like a game to them, but that doesn't mean you can't strategize ahead of time and try to—in some cases, quite literally—soften the blows.

A stairgate (or two) is a must! There's no real downside to having stairgates, so keep them up until your child is at least four or five as an extra precaution, and always make sure you're with your child when they climb up and down the stairs. You never know when they'll lose focus and need you to catch them.

Now, let's talk about that furniture that you lovingly picked out when you moved in. The day you decided to have a child, that furniture became a diving board for your toddler to throw themselves off, and they're going to try! That high-top table doesn't seem like such a great interior design choice now, does it?

Stopping them from doing this is nearly impossible, but you can minimize the damage by keeping any furniture your child can climb away from any windows or doors to prevent any daring escape attempts. Your house is now Alcatraz, and you're the new warden. The only difference is you give bedtime kisses to your prisoners.

Dad to dad, honestly, I'd also just embrace the fact that your toddler is going to take an occasional tumble. Focus on teaching them the resilience needed to dust themselves back off again, rather than attempting to wrap them in cotton wool!

Taking Your Toddler Out

Even if you have the best-behaved toddler on the planet (lucky you), you're going to want to be extra vigilant when heading out! Your toddler is going to want to explore, and so they should! Just be wary of them slipping away, chasing dogs, or simply deciding to follow their own path.

One way to deal with this, which I found particularly effective, is using toddler reins. You may roll your eyes at this, but trust me. Once your toddler sees a toy they want, or a candy they like, they'll become an Olympic level sprinter. The best way to rein them in? Well…reins!

They can take some to get used to (for you both), but if your child is anything like my first, reins will be the only way to keep them in your sight!

If your toddler is old enough and able to understand, you could also agree on a meeting point in case they get lost, as an extra precaution. Teaching them to find the customer service desk at your usual grocery store, in particular, can come in handy!

Keeping Your Kitchen Safe

Your kitchen can be a bit of a death trap, and it's filled with things that can potentially harm your toddler. The worst thing is that most of these dangers are shiny too!

Be careful with hot drinks, keeping them away from the edges of your surfaces; remove any tablecloths that they could pull to the floor—along with everything on top of them; and put safety locks on your cupboards and drawers to keep little hands off of your utensils!

The only potentially dangerous thing that should be going on in your kitchen is your cooking. What? You expected me to write a whole section about kitchens and not throw in a lame dad joke about cooking? You should know me better by now!

Trust Them

We'll end on a fun one that, let's be honest, is a bit of a contradiction. No, you can't technically trust your toddler, but you *should*; trusting them and allowing them to explore—in a safe and supervised environment—is the only way that they'll show you what they can and can't do!

Trust them to do the right things, such as sharing, and allow them to make mistakes, such as throwing themselves from the couch; just be there to catch them when they do!

Remember that by the time your child is a toddler, they're becoming their own person, and they don't need to have everything done for them like when they were a baby. Be sure to have Kleenex ready for when this happens. The first time they don't need you for something you will bawl. Don't worry, Dad. Happens to even the manliest of us.

It's perfectly safe to give them a little bit of loose, well-monitored control.

Next, we'll take a look at some feeding and nutrition strategies, both for babies and toddlers!

Chapter 5:
Feeding and Nutrition

If parenting books were realistic, they'd be like, "You're going to be scraping food remnants out of a high chair every day for the near future and you'll probably want to cry about it."

- Anonymous

Next, we'll look at some feeding and nutrition strategies, starting with babies and moving toward the toddler age. We'll even look at some ways that we can help our fussy eaters!

Babies

Let's start with our babies, shall we?

Feed On Cue

Bear in mind that most babies will want anywhere from 8 to 12 feeds every day, which is about one every two or three hours. They're sort of like the mogwai from the movie *Gremlins*. And boy, oh boy, will you be feeding them after midnight for sure!

I used to make sure that I had a bottle well-prepared by every two-hour mark so that I didn't have to scramble around while the kids were yelling at me for their milk.

However, we should let babies show us when they're hungry—putting their hands to their mouths, smacking their lips, and sucking their fingers—as this is important for their early communicative skills. That way, they learn that we can recognize their cues and are encouraged to keep communicating.

Once your baby stops sucking or turns their head away from the bottle that could mean that they are full, but they might also just be taking a break or need to be winded, so don't take the bottle away immediately. You ever been to a buffet and needed a moment to catch your breath between your fourth and fifth helpings? It's like that, but for babies!

Burp your baby by sitting them up on your lap, or laying them over your shoulder, and gently patting them on the back until they're done!

If they're still turning their head away when you offer the bottle again, then they're full!

Having a bottle-making schedule will give you less to stress about, as well as prevent your baby from getting too stressed. Just make sure that if other family members are babysitting, you ask them to do the same to keep things nice and consistent.

Supporting Your Partner

Breastfeeding can be a big decision for your partner, and though you'll have your own opinion, it's important that you allow them to make the final decision.

Breastfeeding can be a tough experience that exhausts women and leaves them in physical pain, and the reality is that breastfeeding isn't the be-all and end-all. There's nothing wrong with formula-feeding your baby.

For those whose partners do choose to breastfeed, remember that they should be expressing milk too, so there's no excuse not to do your share of night feeds!

Be Prepared for Day Trips With Ready-to-Drink Formula

Day trips with your baby should be great opportunities to

bond with them, connect as a family, have fun, and make memories! Unfortunately, there is nothing that's more annoying than having to make up formula and cool it back down when you're on the go.

That's when you run to your nearest corner store, grab some Diet Coke for your baby and -

No, no, no, I'm joking, are you serious? But what does come in handy is ready-to-drink formula!

Ready-to-drink formula only has to be warmed slightly, and it can be poured into a sterilized bottle before being fed to your baby right away. You can even leave the sterilized bottle in a bottle warmer to keep it at the right temperature.

Some ready-to-drink formulas even come with a teat, completely negating the need for a sterilized bottle at all and making things even easier!

Just bear in mind that once they've been opened, bottles of ready-to-drink formula need to be refrigerated and used the same day. As a result, my advice is to use one per feed, and only use them when you can't get your hands on any boiling water.

Do yourself a favor, and pack a few of these for your day trips!

Structured Sterilizing

Before you know it, you'll be surrounded by baby bottles that are dirty, clean, sterilized, unsterilized, and of all manner of shapes and sizes. If that sounds like chaos, that's because it is!

Sterilizing is important, but it's not something you should drive yourself mad over. Bottles should be sterilized once before use. But if you drop one onto a clean surface after sterilization, wiping it with a baby wipe is fine, rather than starting over again!

I took ownership of a sterilization system that looked something like this:

1. Rinse the used bottles immediately, or as soon as possible, to prevent the milk from drying and solidifying. When that happens, it's both disgusting and annoying.

2. Each evening, sterilize the bottles that you've used that day so that you have a fleet of clean bottles ready for the next day.

3. If you're feeding your baby different volumes of milk throughout the day, make life easier for your sleep-deprived self by allocating each amount to a different

colored bottle.

Introduce Mashed Foods Slowly (From Six Months)

When your baby reaches six months of age, it will typically be safe to start introducing them to new textures and flavors. This time is really fun, and it's amazing to see their eyes light up because of new tastes.

I recommend mashing up the following:

- cooked parsnips

- potatoes

- yams

- apples

- sweet potatoes

- broccoli

- baby rice mixed with their milk

Just remember to blend it into a smooth paste to prevent any choking! And we know you'll be curious to see what mashed broccoli tastes like. Go ahead, try it Dads. I won't tell anyone you're eating baby food I promise.

Also, be mindful of any foods that may cause an allergic reaction. The foods below are known to be common allergens:

- cows milk

- eggs—these should never be served raw or lightly cooked)

- foods with gluten (barley, rye, and wheat)

- nuts or peanuts—these should only be served ground or crushed until age four

- seeds—they should also only be ground or crushed

- soy

- shellfish—never serve it raw or lightly cooked

- fish

Introduce these foods in small amounts, one at a time, so that you can easily pinpoint the root of any adverse reactions. Please also bear in mind that babies aren't allowed honey until they turn 1, as the bacteria inside it can cause serious illness!

As tempting as it might be to only serve your child sweet veggies like sweet potato, remember to serve the likes of cauliflower, spinach, and broccoli too, to ensure they get used to a range of flavors!

Toddlers

Consider Their Appetite and Hunger Levels

Most toddlers' appetites will be hard to plan around, given that they will be fluctuating within different growth spurts and that some days they will expend a crazy amount of energy.

It's not uncommon for a toddler to follow a day of gluttonous feasting with a day of picky eating that makes you want to scream "But you liked carrots yesterday!?" into your own dinner.

This can be even more of an issue at dinner time, when you're worried about sending your toddler to bed on an empty stomach.

Let me give you a quick bit of reassurance before we go any further: If your toddler is hungry, they'll tell you. Even if that comes in the infuriating form of ignoring their dinner and wanting snacks, or them telling you T-minus three minutes before bedtime, you'll know that they're hungry!

Of course, when they're acting out and wanting snacks for every meal, that should be dealt with very differently, and we'll look at a strategy to deal with that later on. But when it comes to their hunger levels, some things that you can do throughout the day to prevent them from disrupting their body's hunger signal include:

- stopping them filling up by drinking too much.

- keeping an eye on their energy levels and serving dinner a little earlier if needed.

- limiting snack intake—although, if your toddler isn't hungry because they've been scoffing strawberries, it isn't the end of the world.

I know the quick, mid-day trip to McDonald's is tempting, but think about the ramifications it could have on their appetite later. But the best part about being a parent? You can totally sneak that Big Mac when they're asleep. Isn't being an adult awesome?

Dealing With Food Refusal

Okay, you're hot and sweaty, having made dinner after a hard day at work. You're tired and hungry, and all you want to do is settle down and eat. Unfortunately, your toddler has different ideas and straight up refuses to eat what you've served them.

Now you may want to fling the plate at the wall and refuse to cook anything outside of a microwavable TV dinner again, but that's not really gonna fix the problem, is it?

You've prevented them from drinking too much, their energy levels are fine, and you've limited snack intake. What now?

First, bear in mind that the moment you force your toddler to eat, you've lost the battle, as this is an age group in which most kids will become incredibly stubborn and dig their heels in. Second, avoid bargaining with them—such as suggesting that they "eat half"—as doing so is giving into their stubbornness. Third, never offer dessert as a prize once they've finished, as doing that will essentially tell them that their dinner is inferior to the ice cream that they're going to have after; I'm aware that it is, but we don't need to tell *them* that!

Consider what you are serving them: Is it something that you *know* they like? Is it a favorite of theirs or something that they've eaten well before? If so, they might be simply testing your boundaries and learning from your reaction.

If so,

- stay calm.

- don't force them.

- make sure they have cutlery and a chair that they're comfortable with.

- turn off all screens.

- be a role model and eat your own dinner.

- remind them that they won't be offered anything else.

If you're offering a new food, that they might be unsure of, do all of the above, but also consider:

- whether they simply don't like it.

- offering them some familiar foods with the new ones.

- starting with small servings.

I'd never recommend starting with big servings of a new food, as the risk of you being left with your head in your hands is too great!

Make Food Fun

We all love food, don't we? That shouldn't be any different for your toddler!

Allow your toddler to explore food, both at mealtimes and away from them. Forget about mess, and allow them to experiment with new textures and tastes, whether it's playing with mashed potatoes or making art from pasta shapes. Make sure your toddler sees food as a source of fun, which will only increase their chances of trying new foods. And hey, whose to say you can't join in? You're just dying to make a mashed potato sculpture, aren't you?

You can also create games around food to teach them about nutrition, practice their cutlery skills, and even get them involved in the preparation of meals.

A few things that I found beneficial were

- letting my kids wash vegetables.

- letting them butter bread and make sandwiches.

- using stencils to cut vegetables into shapes to teach about both shapes and healthy eating.

- teaching the kids about cutting, stirring, and pouring (with toddler-safe utensils).

- emphasizing the importance of washing their hands and having good hygiene.

Another thing that was both fun and beneficial was the simple act of sharing food together. Nachos with long stringy cheese and lots of messy dips was especially fun.

You could also make dinners more fun by arranging your toddler's plate creatively, such as creating a smiley face out of their fruit and vegetables or using stencils to turn their ingredients into fun shapes.

Try serving their meals on fun, colorful plates! You may like it so much, those fun plates will become a staple for every dinner you have from here on out. Just remember to switch back to regular plates when hosting company...

I can't stress enough how effective it can be to put a plastic sheet down and forget about all of the mess until you're done. Oil cloth can be bought at most craft or fabric stores and makes for a perfect, wipe-able, foldable surface. And even if things stray beyond this safe zone, mashed potatoes up the walls are a small price to pay for a toddler with a varied diet who will grow into an adult with a healthy relationship to food!

Taster Plates

Let's talk about fussy eaters and why they are fussy in the first place.

Most children that are fussy eaters, aren't being fussy to stress you out or be naughty—although it will definitely feel that way at times! They're actually just reaching an age where they are becoming more independent and seeking control.

With that in mind, I have a great way that you can give them some of the control that they want, while keeping your head and preventing you from making four different meals: taster plates!

Taster plates are little dishes of new foods that they haven't tried yet or aren't sure of. These can be given alongside their dinner, but in the beginning, I'd recommend offering them outside of mealtimes to minimize any pressure your toddler feels. The more your toddler feels that trying new foods is a fun choice rather than a demand placed upon them, the easier it will be for them to reach for novel items.

Just put the new foods down, leave them out, and walk away, or continue playing with your toddler. Don't even ask them to eat it; just let them know what the food is, and assure them that they can give it a try if they want.

Have a few bits yourself to show them it's nice, and then, leave them to make their own decision, giving them a little of the control that they're craving.

Get Your Toddler Involved

One of the main issues that toddlers have with food is that they find all of the options intimidating, and who can blame them, there are a lot of them! Have you been to a grocery store lately? There's like twenty different kinds of cheddar cheese for sale. I'm siding with the toddlers on this one, it can get overwhelming fast!

A great way of demystifying some of their intimidation—as well as encouraging them with a little more of the control that they're so desperate for—is to get them involved in not only the preparation of their meals but the selection of them too.

I'm talking about everything! Start with shopping for ingredients and letting them choose the produce they like the look of the most. Just try and limit them to three options to prevent overwhelm. And you may want to steer them away from the candy aisle, unless you want chocolate for dinner every night. Actually…that doesn't sound too bad!

Next, offer your toddler a choice of three meals that you can make with their chosen ingredients. Don't worry if a meal itself is a bit weird; the important thing is to provide that sense of complete ownership over the decision that your toddler is so desperately craving. And who knows? Maybe their odd concoction will be good. Peas and carrots doused in pasta sauce may just be the next big thing in the culinary world.

Once they have made their decision, be sure to get them as safely involved as you can in the kitchen. From getting the ingredients out of the cupboards and fridge to washing the fresh produce that they chose or tossing the salad that's made with it, every step helps to familiarize your child with foods and get them excited to taste the results of their hard work.

Once everything is made, make sure to serve the meal to the whole family, rather than just your toddler, and watch them beam with pride as you all tuck in together.

Make Mealtimes About Much More Than the Meal

Mealtimes can be a highly stressful and pressurized time for both toddler and Dad, so try to make them about much more than just the meal.

If there's one thing that most toddlers have in common, it's that they like to chat, so indulge them, and make dinner time, chatting time. Don't worry too much about how slowly they're eating; just focus on how comfortable you're making them feel so that they associate dinner with having a nice time with the family, rather than feeling like it's a time that they're forced into.

One of the simplest ways to remember this strategy is to remind yourself that a toddler that has all eyes on them because they're talking is much more likely to eat their meal than one that feels over-observed because they're being forced to eat.

In Chapter 6, we'll look at some strategies to help us develop our bond with our children.

Chapter 6:
Bonding and Development

Don't handicap your child by making their life easy.

– Robert A. Heinlein

This is where we start to focus specifically on our toddlers and look at some strategies to help us bond with them, as well as to support them in developing personally.

Give Them the Independence They Need

Most toddlers are going to go through a tidal wave of emotions as they develop. All of a sudden, they want independence and space from their daddy to do things by themselves. They might want to dress themselves and even play on their own. At the same time, they might fear you leaving or not being within close proximity.

They're going to be torn between the fact that they are becoming their own little person and that they want Daddy around! Both of those things are okay, but they will make things complicated for our little ones.

It's important, during this time, to give them the healthy independence that they are seeking and show them that you trust them, while always being close enough to keep them comfortable.

Just as with their diet, one way that you can help validate their need for independence is by letting them make decisions, such as choosing what outfit they would like to wear. Sure, they'll be walking out of the house in a cowboy hat, fairy wings, and rain boots, but good taste is all subjective, no?

This can be difficult for us dads, to be honest, because for many of us, it feels as though they go through from needing us for everything to being ready to take on the world alone overnight.

Just remember not to take it personally. Their independence is a crucial part of their development, but they're always going to need Daddy! (Especially in 18 years when they're at college calling for cash. So you always have that to look forward to, Dad!)

Validate Their Feelings

Your toddler is going to really start to recognize their emotions around this time, which is going to lead to some crazy tantrums and some tear-filled meltdowns that will leave you a little lost.

Remember that to a toddler, the little things are big things. So, even though the fact that they dropped their banana in the sandpit might not seem like a huge deal to us, for them, they lost their tasty snack that they'd been looking forward to, and that's devastating. And if you've ever lost a snack you were craving all day, you'd know the pain is real.

My advice is to always validate how they feel, rather than making them feel unjustified in their response or otherwise dismissing their experience. For example, you might be tempted to assure them that "It doesn't matter, we have more bananas at home," but what you're essentially saying is that they shouldn't be upset.

If you instead told them, "It's okay that you're upset about your banana. It's tough not to have something you wanted to enjoy. It can make us sad or even mad, but when you're feeling better, we'll have a nice time, and we can have another banana when we get home." You're then assuring them that what happened is upsetting, but you're also reminding your child that they can still have a nice day.

This approach not only teaches them that how they feel is important but also helps them learn the resilience that they need to respond to feeling upset in a healthy way. Have you ever had a buddy tell you "It's okay the (insert favorite sports team) will do better next season. Just wait!"? It made you feel better, didn't it? Even though it's sometimes not true at all.

Toddlers are also able to start feeling empathy, so you could also give them an example of something that made you feel upset. This can make sure they feel even more understood and that they understand that even adults get upset.

It's not all doom and gloom either, feed into their positive emotions too, and mirror their enjoyment back to them. Let them be excited, happy, and bouncing off the walls! Join them, and never dampen your toddler's enthusiasm for anything.

Label Your Household

A good strategy that can help your toddler learn the names of things and improve their reading skills is to label some of the things in your house that your toddler uses the most, such as the fridge, the sofa, and the chairs for example.

I already know what you're thinking: The last thing you want is loads of labels stuck all over the house. Don't worry; the idea is that every month or so, you rotate the labels so that your child learns the names of lots of different objects without becoming overwhelmed. This allows you to avoid just sticking a label to everything all at once.

For consistency, use the same labels, and write or type in the same font for each of the objects. Then, use some double-sided tape to stick them to your objects of choice.

Just a fair warning, don't try to stick labels to your pets. They don't love it. Not that I'm speaking from experience or anything of course…moving on!

As your child develops their reading skills, you can start to ask them what letter each object starts with or get them to point out objects that start with a specific letter. Don't be put off if your child isn't reading yet though, keep reinforcing the words, and your child will start to recognize them.

Role Play

If you've ever dreamed of being an actor, now is your chance. Prepare your Oscar acceptance speech because you're about to get cast in the role of a lifetime which is...well, whatever your toddler decides you're playing that day.

Playing make-believe will give them a great opportunity to be just like all of the adults they see in their lives, such as police officers, doctors, teachers, and their daddy. (You might also notice some idiosyncratic behaviors you have that your child has picked up on. You may begin to wonder *Wow, do I really walk like that?*)

This form of play will not only develop their creativity and observation skills but also provides a great chance for both you and your child to bond together.

There's no need for any significant outlay either; just grab some simple dress-up clothes, look for bits and pieces around the house that can be used as props together, and let your toddler create a fun scenario!

Just remember to let them lead the way so that their creativity is encouraged and they are fully engaged.

Like all good improv masters, follow the "yes, and" rule. Even if your toddler, playing as a grocery store cashier, tries to charge you $500 for a single apple.

This strategy is also fantastic if your toddler has an upcoming appointment—with a doctor or dentist, for example—as it will help them know what to expect.

Create a Family Tree

Creating a family tree together is a great way of not only immersing your toddler in arts and crafts but in their family too! Print out pictures of your immediate family, as well as a tree stencil—many of which can easily be found online—and let your toddler color the tree.

Next comes the really fun bit, sticking everyone to the tree! Why not add an extra fun element by asking everyone to send you pictures of them pulling funny faces, ensuring that your toddler smiles every time they see it?

And hey, seeing your siblings and parents look like goofballs is kind of a win for you too, right?

Be sure to add a sticky note to each picture, with the name or title of each family member. This will not only teach your toddler who they are but also help them develop memory and word association skills. The more confident your toddler becomes, the more of the sticky notes that can be removed.

Once their tree is ready, your next job is finding somewhere visible to put it up. I chose my kids' bedrooms, but the living room is a great option as they'll be spending lots of time there too.

It'll give them something fun to talk about at family gatherings. Right before they tell embarrassing stories of you walking around in your underwear to your in-laws. Toddlers haven't really grasped the concept of a 'censor' yet.

Create a Calendar

This activity is great for teaching your toddler about both numbers and the days of the week and month!

Create a calendar grid together out of a poster board, leaving space for you to write the names of the months (in pencil) and for your toddler to decorate and make the calendar their own! Write the days of the week across the top of the board, and then number some cards from 1 to 31.

Next, you should attach some Velcro to the boxes on your poster and to each of the numbered cards. Once you've stuck your poster up at your toddler's eye level, you're ready to go!

Take your toddler to the poster every morning and challenge them to add the correct numbered card to it, talk about what day of the week it is, and what they might do that day.

Doing this every morning will teach your toddler all about the days of the week, months of the year, and numbers. Plus, it will encourage the two of you to spend time together in the morning and discuss the day ahead—sounds like ample bonding time to me!

Scavenger Hunts

Scavenger hunts are not only great fun, but they encourage problem-solving skills, creativity, patience, and focus.

These can be created at home—such as by hiding a treat somewhere in the house—and led by clues that you come up with beforehand. But they can also be created on the spot when you're out and about to keep your toddler engaged. For example, when your toddler is involved at the grocery store, you could encourage them to lead the way and find ingredients based on your description. A carrot becomes much more exciting when it's being found after a toddler-led, store-wide hunt. Pro tip: Write your grocery list in the same order as the aisles of your grocery store so that this is still controlled chaos and your toddler doesn't become demotivated.

Your hunts can be tailored to be less, or more, challenging, depending on the stage of your child's development. If your child is learning colors and numbers, you could challenge them to find three objects of a certain color. Or if your child isn't quite ready for that yet, you could challenge them to find one of their favorite cuddly toys.

Make sure to keep your instructions clear. This will minimize the risk of your toddler becoming frustrated and ensure that they get the maximum benefit from listening to you. If your child isn't showing interest, you could always just pretend you can't find something, and watch them scurry away to help.

And if your kid is old enough you can task them with running to the cupboard and grabbing you a snack of your choosing. What? Why should they have all the fun?

Once your toddler is comfortable enough, the next step may even be letting them create a scavenger hunt for you! You can encourage them to come up with hints and clues, before leading the way for you.

No matter who is doing the finding, you'll have a lot of fun!

Take in Your Town

This activity is a great excuse to get your toddler out and about, learning all about their hometown.

Exploring your locality combines fresh air with educational benefits to create a very worthwhile activity. Grab a packet of index cards, and turn them into "town cards," dedicating each one of them to a landmark in your town. Although you may want to keep it child friendly. You don't need to point out the bar mommy and daddy got kicked out of ten years ago.

Take the cards out with you, stopping at places such as supermarkets, gas stations, police stations, and even historical landmarks. Let your toddler either draw the place or a symbol that represents it.

When you get home, you can then go through each of your cards and discuss each place, who works there, what you would find inside, why you would go there, and why it's important to the town. They will not only learn about the place itself but about jobs too!

Whenever you go out, take the town cards with you, and challenge your toddler to find the right card as you pass places. You can then ask them questions about that place to test their memory. For your toddler, this will turn even the most mundane of trips into a mini adventure and opportunity to learn.

You could even arrange visits to your local police station, fire station, or anywhere that you wouldn't typically go so that they can learn even more. Most of these places will be more than happy to accommodate curious kids if you ask ahead of time. Plus, you may even get to see a fire truck up close! Which is cool for any age. You know I'm right.

Stimulate Their Senses

Toddlers are what's called *sensory learners,* meaning they learn about the world around them through their senses—rather than, for instance, through reading about a topic as they will later in life. This means that they're constantly seeking stimulation of their senses. This gives us dads a great opportunity to teach our toddlers all about letters and numbers, while giving them the stimulation they need.

Start with a poster board, and write some letters and

numbers on it with a dark marker. Grab some textured items, such as cotton balls, sandpaper, pipe cleaners, wool, or whatever you can imagine; just avoid choking hazards, and get a good variety.

Then, help your toddler use safety scissors to cut these items into the shapes needed to cover the letters and numbers. This activity will challenge their cutting and sticking skills and encourage them to feel a wide variety of different textures.

Once you're done, you'll have a great, textured board that your toddler will not only find exciting, but that will also give them the opportunity to feel the shapes of the letters and numbers, and also a reason for you to make use of all the random junk you may have laying around your house. It's a multi-purpose tool, people!

Try to get into the habit of reading the letters and numbers once a day, as your child runs their fingers across them and explores. You could even choose to spell your child's name on the board, adding yet another layer of development for them.

When you and your toddler go out and about, you can point out the letters and numbers from their board on signs, stores, and wherever else you see them.

Radio-Controlled Car Track

This is one of my favorites, and it's a strategy that I leaned on time and time again to "trick" my kids into working on their fine motor skills. Needless to say, you'll need a radio-controlled (RC) car for this one!

There are two ways to implement this one: The first option is to let your child create their own RC track using the things around your house. This could be anything from the laundry basket and clothes to their toys or pillows—anything!

While you have to be able to get the car from point A to point B, your child can make the track as tricky as they like. By letting your child take charge, they'll develop their problem-solving skills, encourage their creativity, and have a lot of fun doing it!

For an added challenge, you could also agree on a time limit, which will also see them become more familiar with the concept of time and numbers.

The other option sees you and your toddler swap roles, with the added bonus of your child working on their fine motor skills as they control the car around your challenging course.

This is an activity that will bring out your inner kid, so be mindful. Before you know it it'll be time for bed, and you'll be asking your partner "C'mon, just one more time? Please? PLEEEEEEEASE?"

Daddy for a Day

Our last strategy is not one for the faint-hearted, or for those of you who saw how fun the RC car idea was, and decided to put this book down and just do that ad nauseam.

Choose a Saturday when you and your toddler have no prior commitments, and simply let them lead you through the day in the same way that you would typically do for them. Now, to prevent anyone coming back and blaming this book when their house is on fire, I'll point out that this strategy should be implemented *within reason*!

No, I'm not suggesting that you let your child flood the bathroom, attempt to cook dinner, or take the car out for a drive; you'll simply let them be the driving force for the direction the day takes.

The day before, tell your toddler that you'll be swapping roles the next day, and then, let them guide you through from wake up until bedtime. It will not only be a lot of fun for you both, but it will also test their memory, leadership skills, and patience.

Giving your toddler this much independence and control will delight them, and providing all goes well, it will give you a valuable incentive to encourage good behavior. Just be sure to set some boundaries on what it means to be daddy, before your three year old puts you in time out.

If you are nervous about throwing yourself and your toddler in at the deep end, you could always start by trying half a day. Trust them, and they might just surprise you.

Just make sure you maintain control over what is eaten by offering them choices, unless you want them to think they can have ice cream for all three meals, which believe me they will want.

We've had some fun in this chapter because bonding with your toddler and aiding their development should be just that—fun!

Next, we'll take a slight turn back to the more serious side of parenting and focus on some strategies regarding behavior and boundaries because no means no! And if you weren't already aware that 'no' is a toddler's least favorite word, they will let you know, and fast!

Chapter 7: Behavior and Boundaries

If you have never been hated by your child, you've never been a parent.

– Bette Davis

Boundaries and rules are really important, and they should be established as early as possible; just prepare for some tears!

The Word "No"

Your child is adorable. Who could ever say no to such a precious little - NO! Get out of that mindset now. Neglecting the 'no' is a big 'no-no', see what I did there? It's only going to make things harder as they get older.

My son was obsessed with the television remote; why wouldn't he be? It lit up and turned on the big, magic box! But he had his own toys and didn't need to play with a "grown-up" one.

It took weeks, possibly even months, of telling him "no" and enforcing consequences that prompted tantrums, meltdowns, and screaming before he learned that I would not budge on this rule. But at times, it simply didn't feel worth stopping him. Thankfully, my son eventually got just as sick of hearing "no" as I got of saying it.

I liked to use a three-strike rule:

1. Changed behavior after one "no" brought praise for listening.

2. Needing two evoked no further consequences.

3. Being told "no" three times, and oh boy, consequences were needed, such as the confiscation of a toy for a few minutes.

But on the occasions repeating myself three times still wasn't enough, it was time for the naughty step, which we'll cover in greater detail later in the chapter.

Consistency is the key!

Raising Your Voice

My dad shouted a lot, and as a child, I didn't really blame him. He worked hard to put food in our bellies, and at times, my siblings and I were complete nightmares. Well, more so my siblings. I was an angel…Okay, that's a bold faced lie.

The problem was that over time, we became numb to the shouting, and it stopped having the desired impact.

By setting boundaries that come with potential consequences and are consistently adhered to, your child will learn the difference between right and wrong and will respect the punishment attached to behaving in the wrong way.

Raising your voice can also raise the stress levels of yourself, your child, and even your partner, which no one needs, let's be honest. Raising a child is already stressful enough, do a favor to yourself, and your blood pressure, by keeping the shouting to a minimum.

See your voice as an invaluable tool when it comes to educating and disciplining your child. If you crank up the volume every single time they are naughty, you leave yourself with nowhere to go and no way of escalating things when they are being particularly difficult.

There's also the added caveat that the less your child hears you raising your voice, the more of an impact it will carry. This can make a slightly raised voice much louder and more impactful than shouting at the top of your lungs—which you shouldn't do, but you might! (Look, sometimes desperate

Behavior and Boundaries

times call for desperate measures)

Save your voice for when all else has failed and you really feel like you need it. Your voice is your superpower, Dad. With great power comes great responsibility. Use it wisely!

United Front

The last thing that you or your partner needs is opposition from each other.

Try to avoid the tennis match of "ask Mommy," or "ask Daddy," and establish a united front early on. This will prevent your child from being confused by different rules or thinking they can manipulate the two of you against each other; you'd be amazed how often young children will start trying to do that, it's like having a 4 year old conman living your home.

Once your child can sniff out an imbalance, or see one of you as "the boss," it will become harder for the other to provide discipline as a result. The last thing you want is to be seen as a soft touch!

A "no" from Mommy or Daddy should be a collective one. You are a team! And like all great teams, you need to work together. You think World Series are won when the pitcher's trying his hardest, and the first baseman is giving an opposing player that chocolate bar the pitcher said he couldn't have? No. Okay, maybe that metaphor was a bit convoluted, but you get the idea.

If your partner has dished out some discipline, make sure your child knows that you agree with their decision. And always resist comforting them when they're crying because they've been scolded. This can be really hard, but if you give your little one a cuddle because they're upset at being told "no" by mommy, it will only undermine her; or vice versa, she could end up undermining you.

If a decision requires discussion between the two of you, make sure you leave the room and do so away from your child to prevent one of you from coming across as domineering. Oh, and your child will only side with who is giving them what they want, which will both be annoying and prevent from you talking without interruption.

The Naughty Step for a Time Out

Feel free to replace the word "step" with a chair, corner, or whatever else you're designating as the "naughty zone."

I know, the mention of "naughty zone" sounds less than pleasant. In fact, it may sound cruel. I'm sure as you're reading this lightning just flashed outside, locusts have manifested in your house, and all your furniture has begun to levitate! Take a deep breath and relax. The "naughty zone" is necessary, and not all that bad. You're going to want it. Allow me to explain.

There will undoubtedly be days when none of the above has worked, your child is refusing to listen, and they need a consequence that is going to get their attention. For my kids, this was the bottom step of the stairs, which provided the perfect mix of visibility (for me, not them) and a quiet space for them to calm down and think about their behavior.

There are two key aspects here: The first is consistency, both with the behaviors that see them taken to the naughty step and the time they spend there. The second is willpower, as in the determination to keep putting them back in that same place time and time again when they keep getting up.

It may exhaust you to keep putting them back, but do not give up Dad! This is a marathon, not a race! Although you may feel like you've just ran a marathon after you've sat your toddler down for the hundredth time in five minutes.

The first few times you implement this discipline strategy, your toddler is going to completely reject it, and what should be a five-minute timeout could easily become an hour-long battle. Stick with it and be clear and concise with your message—for example, "You are sitting here for five minutes because you have been naughty by... (be as specific as you can about their bad behavior)."

If you can, place a timer somewhere that your toddler can see it count down their time on the step. This will also help teach them about numbers. (If they're sitting there they may as well learn something, no?) Just be sure to reset it each time your child gets back up again. Fair warning, those five minutes may quickly turn into twenty. Hope you didn't have evening plans!

This will feel excruciating in the beginning, but with any luck, within a few months, your toddler will understand the consequence of the naughty step and will choose good behavior over a visit to it.

Time Ins

Now that we've talked about time outs, it's time to talk about time ins!

Time ins are similar to time outs, except they're a little gentler and are spent *with* your child. The purpose of a time in is to hopefully avoid a time out entirely by letting you both cool off together and discuss what happened. This provides a chance to teach them how you'd like them to behave in future.

To engage in a time in with your toddler, first choose somewhere neutral, like the sofa or the dining table, and go there together. Once you've both cooled down, put your arm around them, and validate the way that they are feeling—for example, "I know that you're angry because you wanted a snack, but your dinner will be ready in 20 minutes."

Next, you should explain the way that things should be handled differently in future, such as eating their snack when it is offered or being patient and waiting at the table for their dinner. You could even offer to set them a timer so that they can see when their dinner will be ready.

Time ins will probably take some practice, and there will be times when they're unsuitable because your child is too wound up to converse with you. If that's the case, be patient, and give them time to calm down, before trying to talk things through.

Another way that you can increase the benefit of a time in is by establishing a time-in area ahead of time, like a specific cushion, yoga mat, or part of the room that you keep free of toys. Make it clear that this area is for when everyone (including Daddy) is feeling overwhelmed or upset so that your toddler knows where to go when they're feeling wound up.

Just be sure to set a good example by using it when you're feeling overwhelmed too, which will drastically increase the chances of them following suit.

You might surprise yourself when you find that you're using the time-in cushion more than your toddler!

Don't Take the Bait

Sometimes, your toddler is being naughty for a single reason: attention.

As much as we all want to be able to give our toddlers all of the attention they want, it isn't possible, and the independence and patience that your child learns while playing on their own and waiting for Daddy to be free are crucial in their development.

Now that sounds perfectly dandy, but the reality is

sometimes your child will do what they need to to get you to notice them. What's that, you may ask? Oh, just cause complete and utter chaos. Tropical storms have nothing on the destruction from a hell-bent toddler.

Sometimes, the best thing that you can do is simply ignore their behavior and wait for them to stop once they realize it isn't working. This works particularly well when you make a point of praising all of their good behavior as mentioned earlier.

As long as your child isn't doing anything dangerous or breaking anything, just leave them to it, keeping one sneaky eye on them and giving them the chance to stop of their own accord. But if you start to hear glass smashing in the other room? Run Dad, run!

This will save you the stress of scolding them and will also teach them a couple of valuable lessons: The first educational moment is when they learn the consequence of their actions; for example, if your toddler has decided to snap their crayons, they'll soon learn that they don't have any left to color with. The second lesson is quite simply that being naughty doesn't benefit them!

Converse Instead of Confront

On the days when you're tired, achy, and just want a peaceful evening, it can be really easy to escalate your toddler's bad behavior by confronting them and immediately dishing out consequences.

Remember that time-in cushion I mentioned? You may want to go pay it a visit.

However, the second your toddler realizes that they're in trouble, they're likely to become defensive, start yelling, burst into tears, or engage in an unbearable concoction of all three.

Instead of seeking to confront them with punishment right away, see them being naughty as an opportunity to converse with them. Tell them the consequences of their bad behavior continuing, and give them a chance to do the right thing.

By discussing the situation, you're giving your toddler the opportunity to work on their listening and conversational skills, as well as helping them to develop self-awareness and self-regulatory skills. Perhaps even more importantly, you're also giving yourself a chance to listen to them.

When we listen to our toddlers—despite the fact that some of it might sound like nonsense—we're making sure they feel validated and increasing the chance of them talking to us about overwhelming emotions and urges later, rather than just acting out.

When you're listening, look for any patterns in what they're saying. Are they actually expressing jealousy? Were they feeling left out? Maybe, they were frustrated because they couldn't quite master something yet.

Finding out the root cause is a great thing for you, Dad. The more they learn from their actions the less you have to keep putting them on the naughty step. Let's be real, that's a win for both of you.

Be Proactive Instead of Reactive

Grab your Sherlock Holmes hat (oh c'mon, I know you've got one laying around) and get ready to play detective. See if there are any situations that continuously cause your toddler issues, and what about them makes them behave badly. My youngest always struggled with supermarket trips, and for my oldest, it was dreaded birthday parties!

Once you figure that out, it'll help tons. You'll see it was all 'Elementary my dear Watson!' Okay, enough of the corny

Sherlock jokes, let's get serious.

By learning these patterns of behavior, you can be proactive in setting the ground rules for your toddler early on; just don't do it too early, or you'll risk them forgetting! I used to give my oldest boy little pep talks in the car outside of birthday parties and remind him how I wanted to behave, as well as explain the consequences that would arise if he chose to be naughty.

With my youngest, these motivational speeches always happened on the way into the supermarket, with the promise of him being allowed to get out of the cart and help with the shopping hanging in the balance. As much as our children can be chaotic at times, they can also be as predictable as the sun rising in the morning.

You could also pre-empt behavioral triggers by taking a distraction with you. For example, if you know your child hates long car journeys, but you have to go on an unavoidable family journey, taking some toys, a book, or their tablet with you is only going to make your life easier.

And we all know the last thing we need when visiting family is another stressor. At least this one you can control!

Learn their triggers, and get ahead of the game!

Setting Behavioral Boundaries

Behavioral boundaries can be tricky to set with a toddler because they're often running around relentlessly and being distracted every few minutes by something new.

The other problem can be that though you want to set boundaries, you also don't want to dampen your child's flame and prevent them from developing their cheeky personality; I can't imagine anything worse than a toddler walking on eggshells! Unless of course we're talking literal eggshells. You may think that's silly now, but let your kid near the groceries unsupervised just once and it suddenly becomes your yolky reality.

The best way to strike a healthy balance is to ensure that these boundaries are communicated early on and tracked in a way that your toddler can see them. A chart on the fridge with stickers can be used to show your toddler that some behaviors are permissible in small doses but harmful in excess. For instance, if a child can see that consequences come with not putting away more than, say, five of their toys, they will understand that they can play safely and create a small amount of clutter without overstepping the mark.

Likewise, it's important to communicate healthy limits for

talking back. After all, we want them to be able to explore their developing personality, even if that means being a tad cheeky at times; this will allow them to develop their sense of humor and even learn how to set and communicate boundaries of their own.

Honestly, I considered not including this, as some dads may disagree, taking a more authoritative parental approach. But I loved it when my toddlers started showing a little attitude and character, and I'd hate to have restricted it! Plus, if we're being honest, some of the stuff they say is hilarious. Is it stuff that adults couldn't get away with? Oh, absolutely. Does it make it that much more funny? Again, absolutely.

Instead of demanding obedience, clearly communicate the need for and limitations imposed by boundaries regarding manners, talking over each other, back chatting, yelling, and all of the other little toddler tidbits you can imagine. These boundaries can provide breathing room but prevent them from turning into little monsters.

My niece was the sassiest, most attitude-filled little girl you could imagine, but we loved her for it and loved watching her develop into a little lady who was determined to stand up for herself.

It can be helpful to create an attitude chart and stick it to the fridge, letting your toddler design it and choose some "good" and "bad" stickers. You can then work together to apply the stickers depending on the attitude they show throughout the day, and you can help your child use this to choose how to express their emotions healthily.

And remember, you can always laugh with your partner about the less-than-polite, but equally humorous, stuff your child says when they're not present as to not encourage it. Just because you're a parent now doesn't mean you can't have a sense of humor.

Redirecting or Distracting

Sometimes, the easiest way to prevent bad behavior is to do your best impression of a magician and redirect their attention to take away the source of their frustration or the temptation to be naughty. And if buying a literal magic trick kit to distract them with is the solution, go for it. Sometimes we need all the help we can get.

This can be great for preventing tantrums or meltdowns and is the equivalent of extinguishing the fire before it starts!

Let's say your toddler is pulling books from a shelf, or worse, ripping the pages from them. You could redirect them to a different toy that might help them more appropriately act on this urge or open one of the books up and suggest reading it together to teach them the value of not acting on the urge.

My youngest used to be unable to resist slapping the television when *Bear in the Big Blue House* was on; I think he was trying to pet him, bless him. So, rather than stop him watching his favorite show or spending the entire duration of it in a disciplinary battle, I'd distract him with a soft toy for him to play with while watching it—problem solved!

Positive Reinforcement

We've already spoken a little about the power of championing all of the good that your toddler does, but this strategy specifically relates to catching them not only being good but also resisting being naughty.

So, instead of clapping and giving them a pat on the back for doing a good job, really pay attention to the times that they show restraint. This could be times that they heed your warnings, but more importantly, there will be times that they don't think you're paying attention.

Once your toddler realizes that you are noticing the little things, they'll be much more likely to keep doing them, and you will therefore be less likely to need any of the other strategies above.

In addition to ensuring that our children are emotionally safeguarded and encouraged to grow, it is important to teach them healthy physical self-care habits. In the next chapter, we'll focus on some bath-time strategies to make sure that this vital practice is as fun as it is beneficial for our children's hygiene!

Chapter 8:
Bath Time

When toddlers bathe, they act like they're a junior member of the Summer Olympics diving team. Get ready. By the time you're done, your bathroom floor will have a few inches of standing water. The good news is that wiping up all that water counts as mopping the floor.

– Bunmi Laditan

Here, we will look at the importance of maintaining, establishing, and having a fun bath-time routine for your toddler, as well as strategies to help them acclimatize to the water.

The Bath-Time Routine

Let's start with establishing your toddler's bath-time routine and keeping them safe during it.

In terms of how often you should bathe your toddler, things can vary due to how incredibly messy we all know they can get. If you think you have an idea of how messy your toddler will be, take that amount and times it by three.

As a general rule, two or three baths a week should do the trick, unless they've been out rolling around in the mud, of course, and with toddlers that's definitely not out of the realm of possibility. However, if your toddler takes to the water like a duck and adores bath time, then feel free to bathe them every single day, just remember to use baby oil or lotion once they are out to stop their skin drying out.

When scheduling your toddler's bath time, remember that like with most other parts of their day, it's important that it becomes part of their regular routine. The more ingrained bath time is in your toddler's routine, the safer they will feel, and the more likely they will be to have fun—sounds like a no-brainer to me.

Whether you bathe your child in the morning or at night is, of course, up to you. But I definitely recommend paying attention to what they're more comfortable with and what works best with your household's routines and your child's patterns. I always preferred nighttime baths, as a morning bath followed by watching my son get granola stuck in his hair always stung a little.

Once you've decided on the time of day you're going to schedule bath time, the next step is sticking as close to it as you can and scheduling what's going to happen before and after it too. For example, your toddlers might not have the same desire to fill their hair with granola as mine (they might pick Cheerios), so you may decide that morning bath time is the way to go. If that's the case, simply sticking to a routine of a bath every other day after getting up, followed immediately by breakfast, might be enough to make your toddler comfortable.

Bath-Time Safety

Some of you might already know some of the following advice, but I'm sure you'll agree that when it comes to our toddler's safety, it's better to be safe than sorry!

Let's start with the temperature and level of the bathwater: The temperature should be nice and warm but not too hot. I recommend testing the water on your wrist and giving the tub a good swish before putting them in it, in case of hot patches.

The water level should be no higher than your toddler's belly button when they're sitting down, and a general rule is to bathe them in as little water as you can, while still using enough water to give them a good clean! It's not only safe, but helps you with the water bill. You're welcome!

Preparation is key here; put a rubber nonslip mat down before every bath, and always gather everything you need so that you aren't tempted to dart in and out of the room once they're in the water. In particular, don't forget their clean clothes; it's easily done.

Position your toddler with their back to, but as far as possible from, the taps. This will help them resist the urge to play with them. Trust me, they're going to want to.

When you clean them, do so from top to bottom, starting with their hair, and if you're anything like me you'll still be finding granola from that day's breakfast. While sure, there are some scientific explanations about bacterial transfer that can back up the need for this, the true reality is that most children will *hate* having their hair washed, and starting with it gets it out of the way so that you can both relax!

Lastly, try to keep baths to no more than 15 minutes in length and always apply lotion after their bath to prevent the risk of their skin drying out (*Toddler Bathtime Guide*, n.d.).

The Dreaded Hair Wash

This strategy will focus on toddlers who are averse to hair

washing, but it will also be really helpful for anyone washing their toddler's hair for the first time. It may even help prevent a fear developing in the first place.

To adults, hair washing is nothing more than maybe a boring part of hygienic upkeep at worst. To some toddlers, however, it's like being waterboarded. Or at least that's what they'll make it sound like as they scream to high heavens, the little drama kings & queens.

If you know that your toddler is already anxious, reminding them that they are going to have a bath soon—and that you are going to wash their hair—will allow you to ease their stress and reassure them. It allows them to know what's coming, which is leagues better than randomly pouring water on their head when they least expect it. Trust me, that technique is no bueno!

You could even draw pictures or create a story together about why it's important to wash our hair that you could then use later in the bathroom.

Something that I found particularly helpful was letting my kids wash my hair first. Once they saw that Daddy was fine, some, albeit not all, of their fear was alleviated. I should warn anyone who decides to do this to make sure your toddlers use the tear-free shampoo on you because they're going to get it into your eyes!

Here's where things get a little subjective. Most baby books at this point would tell you to

1. gently massage the shampoo into the scalp.

2. hold your toddler tight.

3. lower them back into the water.

4. use your hand or a jug to carefully rinse the water away (*How to Wash Your Toddler's Hair If They Hate It*, 2023).

I'm sure the above works—I don't doubt it—but my experience with my eldest saw him freak out and thrash so much once I laid him back into the water that he got water into his face, choked and spluttered, and things became infinitely harder moving forwards.

With my youngest, instead of following those four steps, I simply massaged the shampoo into his scalp, cupped my hand over his eyes, and poured water over his head to wash it away. Did he hate it in the beginning? Yes. Did he get over it quickly? Yes, so quickly in fact that within three months, he was completely in love with bath time, wanted water poured over his head, and would ask to be dunked when we went swimming!

Take Things One Step at a Time

For some toddlers, splashing around and having fun isn't going to be enough to balance their fear of the water, which is the camp that my youngest fell into. In this instance, patience and baby steps are key.

My youngest son was petrified of the water, regardless of toys, bubbles, or a bath seat. He wanted none of it and would ball himself up to avoid the water if I tried to lift him in. So, I broke things down into the smallest steps I could:

1. He watched me in the bath.

2. He played with some of his toys in my bath water.

3. He stood in the empty bath with me, with the overhead shower running over us.

4. He played with his toys in the empty tub alone, with the overhead shower on.

5. After repeating the above step more times than I can remember, my son was then happy to start in the tub alone with his toys, with the shower head on; at this

point, I put the plug in and allowed him to play as the tub filled around him.

6. After a couple of nervous moments, he realized that the water was safe.

7. I let him turn the taps on himself and watch it fill up.

8. He ended up loving bath time so much that he tried to climb into the tub even when he wasn't having a bath.

These incremental steps were key in building his confidence, but they took a lot of patience from both him and me!

Give Your Toddler Control

There's that magic word again: control.

Bath time offers another opportunity to give your toddler a little independence and control, so grab it with both hands! Let your toddler choose what bubbles they would like in their bath; you'll find a wide range of product options that can color their bubbles, add glitter to their bath, or make bath time more exciting in all kinds of other creative ways. My kids' favorites were crystals that sat at the bottom of the tub and popped like popping candy.

There are even bath paints kids can use to make bath time that much more fun! Just a word of caution, they may end up on your walls...and your clothes...and everything within a 5 mile radius of your tub.

Your toddler could also choose their favorite towel, the bath toys that they want to play with, and even the shampoo that they'd like to use. It's worth buying two versions of everything, including towels, just for this purpose.

Next, we're going to talk about independence: Once your toddler is feeling a little grown up, having picked the items for their bath, the next thing that you can do to empower them is give them independence within it. Let them squeeze the bubbles into the bath, squeeze the shampoo, and for those that are able, help you massage it into their scalp.

It's particularly beneficial to let a toddler who isn't keen on the washcloth use it themselves. This control will not only make bath time easier for you, but it will also empower your toddler to grow in confidence and learn about independence and self-care.

Get Splashing

If your toddler is anything like my oldest, bath time is going to be daunting in the beginning, and they're not going to want to bathe. You could give into these fears and just tote around the world's smelliest toddler, but I think there may be some better options.

My first strategy was to make the whole occasion a complete mess, I covered the floor in towels and just accepted that there was going to be chaos. I'm talking soaked towels all over the place, soaked clothes for myself (just take them off), and hopefully, a soaked toddler too!

Going into bath time naked also means that you can jump right in if need be, which can also reassure your toddler that they're okay and make things that little bit more fun. I used to blow bubbles and utilize bath toys too—anything that allowed the kids to see the water as a source of fun, rather than something intimidating.

You may have so much fun, you won't want to get out! Then your partner will have two babies to pry out of the bathroom.

Bath Time Equals Art Time

Everyone knows Michelangelo created his finest works of art

while in the tub! Okay, I totally made that up, but that doesn't mean your child can't get creative while getting clean!

One of the most fun activities that our toddlers can do while bathing is drawing! There are all kinds of fun toys that you can buy—such as soap crayons, bathtub finger paints (like I mentioned before), and bathtub markers—that will let your toddler draw all over the bathroom tiles and get nice and messy. The best part, of course, is that they won't be messy for long!

You can even take things one step further by buying foam shapes that will stick to the tiles when wet so that your toddler can turn your bathroom into a collage. Just remember to take a picture before they wash it all away.

Bath-Time Disco

Bath time can be overwhelming and make your toddler feel anxious and a little trapped. So, why not make sure that they associate both the bathroom and the bathtub with disco time for them and their daddy?

There are lots of bath toys that glow and flash, turning your bathroom into a rave, and better yet, you can turn most of the lights off and play music too! An awesome part about this rave is that there's not an egregious cover charge at the door, or overpriced drinks! Woo!

I found this worked best as a reward after they were clean, so we would get all "boring" bits out of the way first; then, it was disco time!

One of the most rewarding elements of this strategy was taking my eldest to the store and watching him pick out toys specifically for the bath-time disco, even though he'd previously hated the thought of even getting his ears wet.

Of course, once he had his toy, he had no problem getting into the bath, and he was ready to endure the cleaning routine so that he could use his new toy to turn the bathroom into a light show!

Just make sure that things aren't so dark that you can't still safely see your toddler, but maybe just dark enough that they can't see your horrible dance moves. Hey, don't worry. Corny dancing is a rite of passage for dads everywhere!

Turn the Bathroom Into the Kitchen

Bath time is a great opportunity to give your toddler some hands-on time with some of the kitchen utensils they've been eyeing up. Tools like the colander are great for water play. Using mixing bowls and spoons will also allow your child to get creative with the water and work on their fine motor skills at the same time.

If your toddler is struggling to get to grips with their cutlery, why not introduce it to the bath and allow them to practice on some sponge? This also presents a great chance for some more role play and for you to teach your toddler about some cooking techniques by copying what they've seen Daddy do in the kitchen; just do your best to stop your toddler from drinking the bath water.

My kids both used to love watching the water pour through the holes of the strainer, but the overwhelming crowd favorite was whisking some of their bubble bath up in a mixing bowl and watching their foamy creation come to life.

Drying and Brushing

Once your toddler is out of the bath, you're presented with a different challenge entirely: drying them and brushing their hair.

The last thing we want to do is chase a naked toddler around the house with a towel and hair brush, so let me give you some tips to avoid that altogether.

The first thing that you should do to make things a little easier is condition their hair while they're still in the tub, especially if they have hair as curly as my kids.

You should also use a child-safe detangling spray after conditioning and before gently combing, the latter of which I recommend doing while they're still in the tub and happily distracted.

When it comes to drying, I used to use the hairdryer at a low temperature—always check it on your wrist first. This not only avoided annoyingly ruffling their hair with a towel, but it also helped relax the kids and send them to sleep.

If you prefer to use a towel, I recommend getting your toddler involved as soon as you can and turning hair drying into a game, either by playing "peek a boo" or incorporating some tickling as you dry.

Most toddlers aren't going to want to sit still for long enough to have their hair dried fully; just remember not to take them outside with wet hair to prevent them getting a chill!

Celebrate Bath Time

It's important to not only make bath time fun but to also treat the completion of it as a big deal, especially if your toddler isn't keen on it!

You'll want your child to develop a healthy relationship with their hygienic health at a young age, that they will carry with them as they get older. Just wait until they hit puberty, you'll be remiss if they don't like bathing BIG TIME.

Make sure you champion them afterward, giving them a big cuddle and providing them with positive reinforcement to encourage them for next time. That way, even if bath time has been a bit of a nightmare, their lasting memory of it will be that you were proud of them.

You could even agree on a small prize for after bath time; just be sure not to paint yourself into a corner, and only offer something that you're comfortable offering time and time again. For example, you might suggest 10 extra minutes of reading time before bed if they're good in the bath or an extra, healthy snack with their breakfast. Anything more and your toddler may take advantage. Remember, they have those manipulation skills. They're like used car salesmen in Pampers!

Some parents think raising a child is a cakewalk as long as you read a few parenting books before birth. To that I say: That's funny! Tell another one!

But let's face it: Parenting isn't always a smooth journey, and at times, every single one of us will become overwhelmed or make an ineffective choice. As a result, in our final chapter, we'll take a look at some personal strategies to help us keep our cool on the days that we're struggling.

Chapter 9:
Keeping Cool

When I'm not sure how to support my child, I focus on my own regulation.

– Anonymous

Our last chapter will look at ways that we can keep our cool and ensure that we don't become overwhelmed, even when our children seem determined to drive us up the wall; we've all been there, don't worry!

Start the Day Right

If you don't get enough "me time," you aren't giving yourself a fair shot at keeping your cool when things blow up. Despite popular belief, parents are people too! Shocking news, I know.

Starting your day "right" is subjective, and so, your morning routine should be dictated by your personal tastes. But one thing that we should all do is wake up at least 30 minutes before the rest of the house does to allow ourselves to ease into the day. It doesn't matter what this looks like; it could involve 30 minutes of exercise, 30 minutes at the dining table with a newspaper and freshly squeezed orange juice, or even 30 minutes of sitting in bed on your phone (hey, no judgments here).

By getting up early, you're doing so on your own terms, taking control of your day and your stress levels immediately. I know that extra time in bed might feel precious, but I assure you, it's pointless when you're woken up by a toddler screaming for their breakfast, or quite literally landing on top of you. For some reason toddlers are like little pro wrestlers and you? You're their opponent.

When the kids were still very young, I liked to take 45 minutes in the morning to myself. My routine consisted of a cup of tea, washing up any dishes that I couldn't be bothered to deal with the night before, and preparing breakfast for the kids ahead of time. Once that was done, I'd honestly just enjoy the silence while it lasted.

That sense of control and peace ensures that you're tackling the stresses of the day from a level-headed place, rather than starting the day with an elevated stress level right off the bat.

Contrast the difference between enjoying a hot drink and preparing your children's breakfast in silence and wrestling to get to the kettle and make the breakfast while your toddlers swarm around your feet—enough said!

Prioritize Self-Care

The easiest person to neglect when running around after everyone else is yourself.

Once you start to slide down that slippery slope, it can become hard to stop your descent, and quickly, things like hunger, tiredness, and the fact that we're being overworked will stack up and weigh heavily on us.

The problem is that a lot of the baggage that we try to carry is in pursuit of becoming a *better* parent. Yet, ironically, it negatively affects our parental abilities when we tell ourselves things like, *I can work three jobs and fit the school run in, I haven't got time to eat,* or *I'll take a break once the kids are in bed.* You may think you're SuperMan but realistically you're a human being just like everyone else. And that's okay! Besides, SuperMan has to fight bad guys all day, who wants to put up with that? Not I!

When we reject our need to take a breath, we make it nearly impossible for us to keep cool in the face of even the smallest sign of bad behavior.

Despite what society may tell us, putting yourself first—yes, even ahead of your children, at times—does not make you a bad parent. In fact, quite the opposite is true, as a happier and better-rested daddy is going to be a more effective one!

Pay just as much attention to your needs as you do those of your children and spouse. When you need some time to yourself, take it, even if that means reaching out to ask for help from your spouse, family, or friends.

Talk Through Your Stress

My first step, when I was ready to blow, was to talk things through with the toddler who was acting up. Full disclosure: As we discussed in Chapter 7, this will have varied results, depending on the emotional state of your toddler and the stage of their development.

That being said, toddlers can have a much greater capacity for empathy than we realize, and telling your toddler that "Daddy is really upset now because of your naughty behavior" can be much more effective than you might think.

Talking things through not only teaches your toddler the consequences of their behavior, but it also allows you to verbalize and release the negative feelings that have reached the boil.

Where your emotional response is still too activated to effectively communicate with your child, alternatives to this include talking things through with someone else or even just talking them out aloud—the ability to record voice notes on my phone has been a true gift when I just need to vent.

Try to view your stress as an overboiling pot on the stove and talking as the equivalent of taking the lid off!

Walk Away

When it comes to becoming overwhelmed by a naughty toddler, walking away is the most obvious solution, but it can often be the hardest to do, sometimes because your toddler is literally clinging to your pant leg. When things get too much and your toddler is on their third tantrum of the day, put them safely in their room or playpen, and walk away.

Once you reach boiling point, your child can feel it, and the only thing worse than an angry child is an angry child with an angry parent. Which may then lead to an angry partner, and now the household is angry! Even the dog!

You'll want to scream and shout, and you probably will—that's okay too; the important thing is to take the time to engage in this self-regulation separate from your child. Take yourself away—for instance, by locking yourself in the bathroom with the baby monitor or taking yourself into the garden with a glass of water.

Take a breath, and deal with your own stress levels before dealing with theirs. There's nothing wrong with losing your head, but it's important to recognize that you have. If you live with a partner and they suggest you take a breather, trust that they have your best interests at heart, and don't ever feel like you're letting your toddler down.

I'm going to tell you something that all of us parents know but would often rather not admit: They might not mean to, or even realize it, but toddlers can be utterly awful at times.

I have no shame in telling you that I shed a few tears while on the toilet more than once. I felt like I was out of my depth, and maybe I was, but I regrouped and got through it, and you will too—once you've walked away and caught your breath.

Parent Like Someone Is Watching

Okay, it's time for somewhat of a truth bomb: Most, if not all of us, parent differently when we're around others. Why? Because we can't bear the thought of someone thinking we're getting too angry or doing a terrible job, so we filter ourselves and find reserves of patience that we simply didn't know existed. There's a level of silent competition amongst parents. It's like we're all vying for the same, arbitrary title of "Best Parents in the Cul-De-Sac!" A title that, unfortunately, doesn't even come with a cash prize.

But, guess what? Our over-the-top fear and paranoia that someone will think we're doing a terrible job can actually help us! The next time you feel yourself getting ready to lose your mind, pretend you're surrounded by other parents, or perhaps worse, *your* parents, or even worse than that...your in-laws, and think about how you would handle the situation in those circumstances.

Think about the way that you handled your toddler's last meltdown in the supermarket. Did you scream, yell, and draw more attention to yourself? Did you storm off to go cry into the produce? I, and the store manager, hope not! If you manage your emotions in the supermarket, you can manage them at home too.

What about those parents that you do see screaming at their children and flaring their nostrils? How do you feel when you see them losing their minds? Let's be honest, you shake your head and think *Wow, I would NEVER!* Even though sometimes your one tantrum away from being them. But, is that the kind of parent you want to be, even if you are behind closed doors?

This can be a tough one to master because at the end of the day, most of the time you aren't being watched. So, I have a little trick for you to get started: record yourself.

I'm serious; when you can feel yourself starting to simmer, either use your baby cam, or just film or record things on your phone. This doesn't mean you have to show anyone, but it does mean that when you watch or listen back, you'll be able to critique the way that you handled things and prepare for how to cope with similar situations in the future.

Parent like someone is watching, even if that someone is you.

That's Not *My* Child!

How would you react to your child's behavior if they weren't yours? I imagine you'd handle things a little differently. The next time things are getting heated, imagine that you are your child's teacher or that you're taking care of a friend's child, and act accordingly. Only difference is that you can't just send them home like you would a child's friend. Sorry, Dad!

Think about the way that your friends or a student's parents would react if they found out you were screaming and yelling at their children; I don't think they'd ask you to help out again! In fact you'd probably storm up to the school with the ferocity of some 18th century angry mob! Just hopefully without the pitchforks.

This strategy will also encourage you to think outside the box with regard to discipline. After all, when your friends' children come to play, you know that you can't discipline them the way their parents might, but they still need to know where the boundaries are.

As parents, we can learn from teachers, which I guess is technically their job, as parents. Nowadays many teachers are opting for disciplinary measures outside of screaming and yelling. Which makes me wonder...Where was that rule when I was a kid!?

Observe techniques they use when handling a naughty child. But, try to make sure they're suited for modern times. Banging our fists or sitting in the corner with a dunce cap may have worked in the 1950's, but certainly not today!

This strategy can help you teach your child about the consequences of their actions and support you in resisting the urge to raise your voice.

This skill requires a shift in mindset that can take some practice, but nailing it can be the difference between a stern scolding that resonates with your toddler and the pair of you having a meltdown that ends in tears for everybody.

Breathing Exercises

I know, I know; I can already feel you rolling your eyes. But, just take a breath and relax. Get it? Okay, okay, but breathing exercises fall into the "don't knock it until you've tried it" category, and the best part is that they actually do work!

I won't pretend to have benefitted from all of these personally—after all, any coping mechanism is more suited to some than others—but I have reliably used a couple of them for years now; the rest I've included because I know other dads that swear by them. Try each technique at least twice to determine whether it is worth keeping in your arsenal of adaptive strategies.

The more often you practice these skills while you are calm, the easier they will be to implement when you feel your lid is about to blow off, so stick with it.

Deep Breathing

Did you know that the shorter the breaths we take, the more anxious we make ourselves? When you combine that with the fact that stress itself can make us take shorter breaths, it's easy to see how we can lose control of our breathing and make everything worse.

The next time you can feel yourself getting stressed, try the following (Fowler, 2022):

1. Lay on your back or sit in a chair; the key is making sure your back is well supported.

2. Place one hand on your belly and the other on your chest.

3. Breathe in through your nose so that you can feel

your belly filling with air.

4. Breathe out through your mouth, and feel your belly deflate.

5. If the hand on your chest is moving more than the one on your belly, you're breathing shallowly, rather than deep into your belly. Continue to breathe deeply until you feel your lungs are fully expanding and contracting.

6. Take three more full breaths, feeling your belly gently rising and falling.

Breath Focus

This technique uses visualization to help you relax (Fowler, 2022):

1. Close your eyes.

2. Take a few, deep breaths, fully expanding your lungs.

3. As you breathe in, feel the air that's filling your body, and imagine that it's filled with a sense of calm. Use a word or phrase that you associate with feeling calm, such as "I'm calm, and I can stay calm for my child."

4. As you breathe out, imagine the tension and stress in your body, leaving with your exhaled breath. Say another phrase as you breathe out, such as "I'm breathing out the frustration I'm feeling, so I can focus on parenting."

5. Try to do this for at least 10 minutes, depending on how crazy things are at the moment.

Equal Breathing

This technique is all about breathing in and out for an equal amount of time and progressively increasing the duration over time (Fowler, 2022):

1. Sit in a comfortable chair, or lay comfortably on the floor.

2. Count to five in your head as you inhale through your nose.

3. Count to five in your head as you exhale through your mouth.

4. Repeat steps 2 and 3 a few times.

5. Then, increase the breaths to 10 seconds.

6. Continue going up incrementally as long as you're comfortable.

Progressive Muscle Relaxation

Progressive muscle relaxation is great for helping us relax both mentally and physically. It targets the muscle groups where we feel tension.

To give it a try, complete the following steps (Fowler, 2022):

1. Lie comfortably on the floor.

2. Relax with a few deep breaths.

3. Tense your foot muscles as you inhale.

4. Release any tension in your feet as you exhale.

5. Tense your calf muscles as you inhale.

6. Release any tension in your calves as you exhale.

7. Work your way up your body, tensing each muscle group as you go, to recognize and release any tension that you find.

This technique will take a bit of time, so it's best to try this while taking some time away from your irate toddler—either as your partner tags in or after putting your child safely in their playpen or room.

Lion's Breath

This technique is great. You get on all fours, crawl around, and roar at everyone you know like a lion. Just do it right now.

Alright, fine. You're not falling for it. But in actuality this technique is a lot of fun, and you can even do it alongside your child. My kids loved getting to do their best lion expression and releasing all of their breath like a loud, roaring lion.

Trying to do this while your toddler is in the midst of a tantrum would be a waste of time and energy, but using it when you can see a tantrum coming is definitely worthwhile!

Follow the steps below, with or without your little monster (Fowler, 2022):

1. Sit comfortably in a chair or on the floor.

2. Inhale through your nose, expanding your abdomen and filling your lungs all the way up with air.

3. Open your mouth as wide as possible and exhale with a "Ha!"

4. Repeat the above steps as many times as necessary until a release of tension is felt.

Again, I know some of you will want nothing to do with any of these. Which is fine, I'm not offended by it. I swear…I'm totally not!

Kidding. But, all I would suggest is that you give at least one of the techniques above a try when you have some alone time; they really work!

Set the Right Example

Your toddler is observing everything that you do, all the time, even when you think that they aren't.

So, when things erupt and your toddler is melting down, reacting to their meltdown with one of your own only teaches them that shouting and getting angry is okay.

The more you shout, the more they'll shout; and the more tense you are, the more tense they will be. Soon, you'll all be shouting and the next thing you know you're getting a call from the neighbors asking you to kindly shut up.

Setting the right example starts with much more than just refraining from shouting, though. Think about your body language: Are you tense and clenched? By softening your body language and relaxing your muscles— lowering your shoulders, unclenching your fists, and uncrossing your arms— you'll send calmer signals to your toddler that might defuse things a little quicker.

One of the first signals that we notice when someone is annoyed is the clenching of the jaw, and your toddler will notice yours too. When you can feel yourself tensing up, think about what signals you're sending and how those signals might be escalating things.

Find Reassurance

When you feel completely defeated and like your toddler is the worst-behaved child in the history of the planet, sometimes the only thing that will make you feel better is perspective.

One of the most comforting ways that I've found to regain perspective is simply to get online and read through parenting forums. There, you'll realize that everyone struggles with their toddler and that it could always be worse. Look, a little Schadenfreude never hurt anyone, okay?

On the days that your kid has decided to cover your television in crayon, there will be someone whose toddler put a broom through the screen! When you're feeling guilty because you yelled and threw the television remote, you'll be sure to find a story of someone who broke their laptop. And then you'll sit back and wonder how they even posted to said forum without a laptop. Before you know it, you'll forget why you were even stressing.

There's no judgment here, dads, none at all; have I thrown things in a rage? Have I come closer than I would like to admit to hitting a door like a petulant teenager? Yes, and yes.

We're all human beings, and once you hear others' stories, you'll soon realize that there's no shame in any of the frustration or anger that you feel. The important thing is learning how to manage it effectively.

Let Yourself Be Angry

I'll quickly give you another timely reminder that shows that this book really is nothing like other parenting books that you've read: Be angry, just not at them.

If you want to scream into or hit your pillow, do it. If you've got a punching bag set up in the garage to let off some steam, have at it. If a stress ball is more your thing, squeeze away!

The worst thing that we can do when we're angry is bottle it up, so do whatever you need to do to release your anger the right way and redirect it from your nightmare toddler.

Act Silly

Things got a little deep as we worked through our last couple of strategies; so, let's end things on a lighter note, shall we?

One of the greatest antidotes to anger and frustration is laughter. So, if you're able to catch things early enough— feeling yourself getting wound up—grab your toddler and do something silly with them.

Fly them around the room, talk in a weird voice, put a pair of their pull-ups on your head, or do the most ridiculous thing that you can think of to put a smile on both of your faces and get you both laughing. You'll be amazed at how quickly that can diffuse things!

Join a Combat Sport

One of the most effective ways to channel your stress and frustration is by joining a combat sport. It might sound intense, but trust me, it's a fantastic way to get a workout, release pent-up energy, and learn some valuable self-defense skills along the way.

Whether it's boxing, Brazilian jiu-jitsu, kickboxing, or Muay Thai, these sports offer a structured environment where you can safely let out your aggression. There's something incredibly cathartic about hitting a punching bag or grappling with an opponent. The focus required for these activities also helps clear your mind of the daily grind, leaving you feeling refreshed and rejuvenated.

Most importantly, combat sports build resilience and discipline—qualities that are incredibly useful in parenting. Plus, it's a great way to meet other dads who might be in the same boat as you, creating a sense of camaraderie and support.

Conclusion

Exhale, you've made it to the end, and hopefully, you've realized that you are far from alone on this journey!

I think I might be tearing up, our time together is quickly coming to a close! I told myself I wouldn't cry!

I hope you're leaving a lot more more confident so that you:

- are comfortable getting involved throughout the pregnancy stage and feel empowered to do your bit, even when you're feeling like a bit of a spare part.

- take your newborn in both hands and bond with them right away, enabling you to establish routines, help yourself and your partner get the sleep you need, and be hands-on with feeding and changing.

- work through the various strategies suggested and nail down the ones that work for you and your child, including discovering the most beneficial options.

- feel confident in keeping your child healthy and safe at all times and in a range of different scenarios, empowering you to spend less time worrying and more time loving!

- have a thorough understanding of feeding and nutrition to ensure your child is getting all of the vitamins that they need to grow and develop, while also making time to feed yourself too.

- are able to develop a bond with your child that both of you can benefit from.

- feel confident and empowered to lay down boundaries that your child will follow and are able to exact consequences for any bad behavior.

- can dive into bath time (pun intended!) and make sure that it is as fun as it is beneficial for your child's hygiene.

- have strategies to fall back on when things are getting on top of you and feeling a little overwhelming.

Try to remember that while the strategies in this book are tried and tested, backed with research—and most have been used by myself personally—they don't take into account the secret sauce or your secret weapon: your gut. No, not the sympathy weight gut, I'm talking instinct!

Use this book as a valuable resource that you can draw from, but always use the strategies as guidelines and listen to your gut!

No one knows our children better than we do, and you'll realize quickly—if you haven't already—that everyone will have an opinion on the decisions you make. Some will feel patronizing, even when they aren't supposed to, and others will feel patronizing simply because they are. The funny thing about raising children is that everyone—including those who have never done it—seems to be happy to be an armchair quarterback. I'd like to see some of them change a diaper while going off two hours of sleep!! It's not as easy as it looks!

Stick to your convictions, trust in the strategies from this book, and remember that there isn't a person in the world who is more invested in your child than you—okay, you and your child's mom.

Be kind to yourself, embrace and learn from your mistakes, and remember that there is no such thing as the perfect parent.

I'll leave you with a quote from my dear mom, who I called in tears after a particularly bad evening, only to be reassured by her promise that, "Son, if you're keeping it together a quarter of the time, you're doing a great job."

Wish you all the best!

References

Adegoke, R. (2023). *Pregnancy quotes for daddy.* Cuddl.
https://cuddl.com/pregnancy-quotes-for-daddy/

Ben-Joseph, E. P. (2018). *A guide for first-time parents.*
Kidshealth.org.
https://kidshealth.org/en/parents/guide-parents.html

Child independence quote. (n.d.). Pinterest.
https://www.pinterest.com/pin/parenting-quotes--
833799318492046410/

Coleman, P. (2017). *New dad survival tips to get you through
the first month.* Fatherly.
https://www.fatherly.com/parenting/new-dad-survival-
tips-first-month

Coleman, P. (2022, December 2). *Why dads gain pregnancy
sympathy weight and how to prevent it.* Fatherly.
https://www.fatherly.com/health/dads-gain-pregnancy-
weight-prevent

Dr. Laura. (2019, August 26). *60 inspirational quotes for new
moms.* St John's Pediatric Dentistry.
https://stjohnskids.com/blog/inspirational-quotes-
about-becoming-a-mother-for-the-first-

time/#:~:text=Quote%20%2356

Eating tips for older toddlers. (2011). Vic.gov.au. https://www.betterhealth.vic.gov.au/health/healthylivin g/eating-tips-for-older-toddlers

Elizabeth. (2023, February 4). *40 toddler & baby eating quotes you'll love.* Shoestring Baby. https://shoestringbaby.com/quotes-about-kids-eating-food/

Feeding your newborn: Tips for new parents. (2018). Mayo Clinic. https://www.mayoclinic.org/healthy-lifestyle/infant-and-toddler-health/in-depth/healthy-baby/art-20047741

Fowler, P. (2022). *Breathing techniques for stress relief.* WebMD. https://www.webmd.com/balance/stress-management/stress-relief-breathing-techniques

Gagne, C. (2020, March 6). *6 most popular baby sleep-training methods explained.* Www.todaysparent.com. https://www.todaysparent.com/baby/baby-sleep/most-popular-sleep-training-methods-explained/

Hanson, K. (2023, April 25). *35 fatherhood quotes that embody the special role of dads.* TODAY.com. https://www.today.com/parents/dads/fatherhood-quotes-rcna80836

How to dress a newborn baby. (2023, June 13). Nhs.uk.
https://www.nhs.uk/start-for-life/baby/baby-
basics/caring-for-your-baby/how-to-dress-a-
newborn/#:~:text=A%20good%20rule%20of%20thum
b

How to wash your toddler's hair if they hate it . (2023, June 5).
Dandydill Way.
https://dandydillway.com/blogs/journal/how-to-make-
washing-childrens-hair-less-of-a-trauma-and-more-of-
a-pleasure

Kashtan, P. (2023). *Your ultimate checklist of baby essentials.*
Www.thebump.com.
https://www.thebump.com/a/checklist-baby-essentials

121 best and inspirational parenting quotes of all time. (2014,
November 7). MomJunction.
https://www.momjunction.com/articles/amazing-
quotes-on-parenting-to-inspire-you_00104303/

Pacheco, D. (2023). *Sleep strategies for children.* Sleep
Foundation.
https://www.sleepfoundation.org/children-and-
sleep/sleep-strategies-kids

Pack your bag for labour. (2020, December 1). Nhs.uk. https://www.nhs.uk/pregnancy/labour-and-birth/preparing-for-the-birth/pack-your-bag-for-labour/

Physical activity guidelines for children (under 5 years). (2018, April 30). Nhs.uk. https://www.nhs.uk/live-well/exercise/physical-activity-guidelines-children-under-five-years/#:~:text=Toddlers%20should%20be%20physically%20active

Smith, V. (2022, March 24). *55+ adorable dad to be quotes.* The Mummy Bubble. https://themummybubble.co.uk/dad-to-be-quotes/

Swimming in pregnancy. (2023). Tommy's. https://www.tommys.org/pregnancy-information/im-pregnant/exercise-in-pregnancy/swimming-pregnancy#:~:text=Benefits%20of%20swimming%20in%20pregnancy,symphysis%20pubis%20dysfunction%20(SPD).

Toddler bathtime guide. (n.d.). JOHNSON'S® Baby UK. https://www.johnsonsbaby.co.uk/bath/toddler-bath-time#:~:text=Generally%2C%20you%20should%20only%20need

Toddlers are a holes quotes. (n.d.). Www.goodreads.com. https://www.goodreads.com/work/quotes/43206221-toddlers-are-a-holes-it-s-not-your-fault

25 things to do when preparing for fatherhood. (2022). Web-Pampers-US-EN. https://www.pampers.com/en-us/pregnancy/preparing-for-your-new-baby/article/preparing-for-fatherhood

Leave Your Feedback on Amazon

Please think about leaving some feedback via a review on Amazon. It may only take a moment, but it really does mean the world for small authors like myself :)

Even if you did not enjoy this title, please let me know the reason(s) in your review so that I may improve this title and serve you better.

From the Author

My mission with this series is to create practical and helpful parenting content that will not only help you maximize your child's potential, but also make your parenting journey as manageable as possible.

I hope that this book was able to help fulfill that mission and provide you with lots of value. Thank you for your purchase!

Don't forget your free gifts!

(My way of saying thank you for your support)

Simply visit **haydenfoxmedia.com** to receive the following:

- 10 Powerful Dinner Conversations To Create Amazing Kids

- 10 Magical Affirmations To Help Kids Become Unstoppable in Life

(you can also scan this QR code)

Made in the USA
Las Vegas, NV
27 November 2024

12833718R00098